Seventeenth Century Prose

Ewing Lectures

SEVENTEENTH CENTURY PROSE

Five Lectures

BY F. P. WILSON

CAMBRIDGE

AT THE UNIVERSITY PRESS

UNIVERSITY OF CALIFORNIA PRESS

Berkeley and Los Angeles 1960

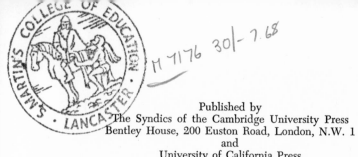

M 7176 30/- 7.68

Published by
The Syndics of the Cambridge University Press
Bentley House, 200 Euston Road, London, N.W. 1
and
University of California Press
Berkeley and Los Angeles, California
Printed in the United States of America

To Joanna

Preface

The first, third, and fifth lectures are the Ewing lectures delivered at the University of California, Los Angeles, in 1958 by invitation of the Committee on Public Lectures and the Department of English. With permission I have added the lectures on Burton and Browne given by invitation of the Department of English in 1953. To Professor and Mrs. Majl Ewing, the generous founders of the Ewing Lectures, to Professor James Phillips, Chairman of the Department of English, and to other friends in the University, I am grateful for many kindnesses and much delightful hospitality.

In the notes I acknowledge a few of my debts, add an occasional comment, and give references to some of the quotations. The spelling of all titles, and of all quotations except those which are set in reduced type, has been modernized.

F. P. W.

Contents

I

A Survey

The seventeenth century has long been recognized as one in which the transition from the medieval world to the modern was greatly accelerated. It is a century in which man revised his conception of the external universe and of his relation to it, revised also his conception of himself and of the powers of his own mind: it is the century of Galileo, Harvey, and Newton, of Descartes, Hobbes, and Locke. The debate of which we hear more and more as it grows older is whether man should obey the tradition or revolt against it; whether he should continue to follow the old guides or should follow new leaders in search of other promised lands. The rationalists slowly win ground, and heresy is no longer solitary and hidden. For some there begins to be a politics without divine law, a religion without mystery, a morality without dogma. It is the century when, in Seeley's phrase, England passed "out of the atmosphere of theology into that of commerce," and what Gardiner called "the mundane spirit" triumphed over Puritanism. Where the emphasis had been upon order and degree, hierarchy and discipline, man's duty to God and the Prince, some now placed it on rights—the rights of the individual conscience, of criticism, of reason. And in the next century there emerges for some a religion of humanity, the belief in a heavenly city upon earth, not indeed in their time but for a not too distant posterity. These changes in thought and belief, for which there had been a long preparation, seem to come to their crisis in the late seventeenth century.

In small things as in great a change is perceptible. In his admirable *Renaissance Guides to Books* Professor Archer Taylor has shown that even in so humble a matter as bibliography there is a break in cultural tradition at the end of the century. In the Middle Ages and long after the invention of printing, when a man could still take all knowledge for his province, universal catalogues of books and manuscripts could be provided with some hope that they might be complete. Conrad Gesner's *Bibliotheca Universalis*, first published in 1545, gave a catalogue "omnium fere scriptorum, a mundi initio ad hunc usque diem," and in his *Pandectae* of 1548 he provided a subject index of all books and all knowledge. We may be surprised at the number and variety of the helps to learning the readers of those days were offered. There was even a list of those books which scholars promise but do not write. It was soon found necessary to print a supplement. The continuity of the tradition is shown by the way in which a new work absorbed and enlarged an old: the Protestant Bale in his catalogue of English writers building upon the Augustinian monk Boston of Bury, and Pits, the Catholic priest, making use of Bale. Historical evaluation was not found to be necessary, and the writers of all ages stood together on one level and in one index. It is as if knowledge was immutable, not to be assailed by the passage of time.

Then, as Professor Taylor shows, about the end of the seventeenth century the old universal bibliographies begin to die off; they are no longer reprinted or brought up to date. Authors of the past, especially the remote past, come to be treated not as authorities, but at most as sources. The first great modern philosophical systems begin to be devised. "Theology, philosophy, and the other liberal arts all start their cultural tradition anew with the eighteenth century." The ancients are no longer regarded as the sum of human wisdom, and the progressive theory of history comes into being, that bad as things may be at the moment they are steadily improving.

So it was at the end of the century, but at its beginning men were far from being friendly to any idea of progress. J. B. Bury and Richard Foster Jones have shown how widespread in Elizabethan and Jacobean times was the belief that nature was decaying, that the moderns had much deteriorated from the ancients physically and morally, that the world was in its old age and nearing its dissolution. On this belief Donne founds much of his *First Anniversary,* and it gives to Raleigh's *History of the World* an elegiac strain—"the long day of mankind drawing fast towards an evening, and the world's tragedy and time near at an end." As late as *Urn Burial* it inspired the Janus-faced Sir Thomas Browne to some of his greatest music.

In England this view was first attacked in an extended argument in 1627 in George Hakewill's courageous and spirited folio, *Apology of the Power and Providence of God in the Government of the World;* but as optimistic and more influential was the message of Bacon. While he held that the world was in the autumn of its days, he believed that to that autumn was appointed the bearing and fructifying of the plant of knowledge. For him the golden age was the last age, not the first. Now Bacon is a smaller man for us than he was for the seventeenth century. For one thing we know so much more than we used to know of the advancement of learning in the sixteenth century, and what we know has not increased his stature as a man of science. Yet it is not easy to exaggerate the influence his doctrines had upon his century: his advocacy of a more searching inquiry into men's minds and motives, his insistence on *fructus* and the useful arts, his antiauthoritarian attitude to the ancients, his optimistic support of the moderns indicated in the very title *The Advancement of Learning,* his passionate belief in the beneficial effects of experimental science "for the glory of God and the relief of man's estate." These doctrines diffuse themselves through the century. Much greater men of science than he was did him homage, and Joseph Glanvill was right to consider Solomon's House in the *New Atlantis* as a prophetic scheme of the Royal Society.

But influential as Bacon was, his disciples later in the century were not in every particular Baconian. The notion that the world was on its last legs dwindled and almost disappeared. Those who did not deny it ignored it. Again, some of his disciples were much more one-sided in their attacks on the ancients than was Bacon. Bacon was neither an "ancient" nor a "modern." Unlike Descartes he did not construct a system which is independent of the past; rather he desired to establish what he called a "sociable intercourse" between antiquity and progress or "proficience." More important for our purposes, his prose style—or rather prose styles, for he had several—cannot easily be squared with the tenets of his followers, whether we think of the aphoristic style of his *Essays,* where the *brevitas* of Tacitus and Lipsius is carried as far as it can go in the English language, or think of the eloquence of many a passage in the *Advancement,* where he is preaching the gospel of science. We should look in vain late in the century for a passage like that in which he praises the durability of learning, look in vain for anything so eloquent or for anything that pays such due tribute to the tradition of learning. I mean the passage that ends:

> if the inuention of the Shippe was thought so noble, which carryeth riches, and commodities from place to place, and consociateth the most remote regions in participation of their fruits: how much more are letters to bee magnified, which as Shippes, passe through the vast Seas of time, and make ages so distant, to partici- pate of the wisdome, illuminations, and inuentions the one of the other?

But in the third quarter of the century the plain style triumphed. It triumphed so completely that elaborate prose was driven out, and for some generations Milton, Browne, and Taylor had no notable successors.

Only by a gross simplification can a revolution so sudden and so complete be attributed merely, or even chiefly, to the new rationalism and the successes of experimental science. The attack on ornate prose came from many different quarters. One of these, to which several contemporary writers drew attention, and some of our older historians of literature, was the tone and temper of the court of Charles II. The court, of course, represented but a small part of the country, though an influential part. There were many writers who did not come within its orbit: the men of science themselves, Boyle, Wren, Newton, Ray. And while we cannot call him a distinguished man of science, there is John Aubrey, a considerable antiquary as later ages have been glad to acknowledge. There are the preachers South, Barrow, Tillotson, who though court preachers kept themselves unspotted from the court. There are the statesmen, Clarendon, Halifax, Burnet, who had access to the court yet did not write for it, but left their memoirs in manuscript for the benefit of posterity. There is the diarist and virtuoso John Evelyn, who never willingly went to court, so he would have us believe, but minded his books and his garden, and found that circle big enough for him. And at the court itself there is Evelyn's friend Margaret Blagge (later Mrs. Godolphin) who contrived to live there, he tells us, the life of a saint. It was felt to be fitting that when she was constrained to act at court in John Crowne's pastoral comedy *Calisto,* she was cast for the part of Diana.

And lastly, right outside these circles whether courtly or learned, completely untouched by the aristocratic tradition of education upon which all these writers were reared, not even a member of the already powerful middle class but of the usually inarticulate peasantry, there is that most articulate genius, John Bunyan.

Yet when we have made all allowances, the fact remains

that the court of Charles II exercised a strong positive influence upon literature and the drama. It is the last English court of which this may be said. Of the nature of this court, its dubious morals and its addiction to the pleasures of each day, its taste for wit and satire and raillery, many a contemporary record tells us. The letter I am about to quote was written from Oxford in 1665 when the court had taken refuge there from the Great Plague of London. Its spirits were far from being damped by the terrors of that visitation.

> There is no othere plague here but the infection of love; no other discourse but of ballets, dance, and fine clouse; no other emulation but who shall look the handsomere, and whose vermillion and spanish white is the best; none other fight then for "I am yours." In a word there is nothing here but mirth, and there is a talk that there shall be a proclamacion made that any melancholy man or woman coming in this towne shall be tourned out and put to the pillory, and there to be whep till he hath learned the way to be mary *à la mode*.

That fits easily into the world frequented by Sedley and Rochester, reported by Etherege, and satirized by Wycherley.

That Charles and his court were arbitrary masters we know from the personal histories of Cowley and Butler, of Otway and Dryden; and when in the last years of his life and of the century Dryden was in disgrace at court and entered into a lucrative agreement with the publisher Jacob Tonson, we feel it to be an important event not only in his literary life but in the history of letters. We can begin to anticipate the time when Johnson could say: "We have done with patronage. . . . When learning becomes general, an author leaves the great, and applies to the multitude." Yet the dependence of the young Dryden upon the suffrages of the court was not entirely harmful. I do not think he is merely using the language of compliment when he acknowledges the court to be the best and surest judge of writing or maintains that thanks to the benefit of converse which the writers of his time enjoyed with a king and court acquainted with the most polished courts of Europe, the solidity of the English nation had been mixed with the air and gaiety of the French. About the time that Dryden was praising the court in the dedication to his essay *Of Dramatic Poesy,* Thomas Sprat, the historian of the Royal Society, was also saying that the English genius was not so airy and discursive as that of some of its neighbors. Humor, wit, variety and elegance of language, he explained, come from frequent conversations in cities, and whereas the French nobility lived close together in cities, the English was scattered for the most part in country houses. Sprat ignored the court, but Dryden did not, could not, ignore the court, and something of the air and gaiety of his prose perhaps he owed to being conversant in courts and keeping the best company. He could hardly have owed them to Tillotson or to the Royal Society. Nor did he owe them entirely to Nature, for his conversation, he tells us, was slow and dull, and his humor saturnine and reserved.

At this point an evenhanded historian ought perhaps to put in a caveat. Before the Restoration there were signs that the fine raillery which Dryden praised and which is as sharply to be distinguished from banter as from railing was beginning to be valued as an instrument of destruction. One illustration must suffice. In late 1659 or early 1660 appeared a translation of Rabelais's *Pantagrueline Prognostication.* To this the translator, a royalist, prefixed a satire on the astrologer William Lilly who for years had made the stars favor the Roundheads and had even prophesied a good year in 1659 for Richard Cromwell. The work is anonymous but is much in the spirit of Milton's nephew, John Phillips, himself a Pantagruelist. "How easy it is," Dryden was soon to observe, "to call Rogue and Villain, and that wittily! But how hard to make a Man appear a Fool, a Blockhead, or a Knave, without using any of those opprobrious terms!" Many satirists there were who were willing to rail at Lilly, to call him rogue and villain, a star-peeping gull, an impudent deceitful colloguing quack, a proditorious fellow, Merlin's brat, a liar of the first magnitude, an audacious atheistical, railing Rabshakeh, and many other opprobrious terms. Not so our translator. He considers Lilly's serious prognostications as if they were on a level with Rabelais's mock prognostications:

> He is such a pleasant Astrologer. And thou resemblest him in this, that although thou art not altogether so good a Droll, yet every man when he reads thee, has a kind of tentation to laughter. And yet thou for thy part seemest so grave and serious that thou wilt easily pardon the Translator of this, having thy selfe so usefully rendred his jest into good earnest: and I know not perfectly whether he were thy Originall, or but an imperfect Type, or faint representation of thee, a greater Prophet to come. Thou hast all along his Style, Figures, and Policy, and all but the profession of Drollery. Thou knowest as well how to wrap thy deceits in a cloud of generalities, that they may not lye open to discovery or reprehension. Do but look upon thy Ephemerides, and thou canst tell us very gravely that some body or other shal dy next month, and as

> plainly foreseest the fall of some great man in August,
> as we mortalls the dropping of a Pomwater in Autumn.
> In fine, thy Prophecies are as sure as Death: for Those,
> as This, are in themselves certaine, but the Time, Place,
> Manner, and Persons, and such petty circumstances,
> altogether uncertain.

This is not railing, and the good breeding of the prose, the quietness of the tone, the easiness of the pace distinguish it from banter. If it is not fine raillery, fine raillery is just around the corner. The dawn is breaking on an age which excels all others in the art of making a man ridiculous.

But to return to Dryden. He was a fellow of the Royal Society—until he stopped paying his dues—and sat on their committee for the reformation of the English tongue. Yet however sympathetic he was at first with their aims, and however much he may have approved of their skeptical way of approach, he cannot have been in full sympathy with their official doctrines on English prose. Or at least he could have agreed only if their precepts were confined to writings about science, to what De Quincey was to call the literature of knowledge as distinct from the literature of power. The society recommended its writers to observe a close naked natural way of speaking, delivering so many things almost in an equal number of words, to avoid the ornaments of language, to prefer the language of artisans, countrymen, and merchants to that of wits or scholars. But Dryden, while he cannot be said to use the language of wits and scholars, as certainly cannot be said to prefer the language of artisans, countrymen, and merchants. His language, like that of any prose writer of good taste in any age, "belongs to human nature as human." As Coleridge said of the language of

Shakespeare, it is "independent of associations and habits from any particular rank of life or mode of employment." For evidence that Dryden does not deliver so many things almost in an equal number of words, does not aim at writing with all the imaginable brevity that perspicuity will bear, we may turn to the essay *Of Dramatic Poesy*. "How artfully," wrote another dramatic critic,

> How artfully the plot of this critical drama is related to the scenic background, so that the very swallows which skim the water ahead of the barge are pressed into service to give a simile for the literary points of some poet under discussion! And by-and-by the watermen are bidden to turn the barge and row softly, that the party may take the cool of the evening in their return; and the talk flows on, as abundant and as richly laden as the river itself.

So A. B. Walkley, and I am tempted to add Denham's famous lines on the Thames which apply so aptly to much of the prose and the poetry of the middle and later years of the century:

> Though deep, yet clear, though gentle, yet not dull,
> Strong without rage, without o'er-flowing full.

Dryden's is a prose of exquisite breeding, of a seemingly natural grace and easy strength, "abounding in knowledge," as Johnson said, "and sparkling with illustrations." If one hesitates to call it "modern," that is only because it is so good.

A profitable way of examining the century's prose is to ask what new forms of writing it required and what changes were found necessary in old forms. Some of the changes which prose undergoes in two very ancient forms I shall be examining in the lectures on biography and on the sermon. An inquiry into what new forms were required will take us back for a time to an earlier part of the century than that I have just been considering.

I have argued elsewhere that the Jacobean age is distinguished from the Elizabethan in its more exact, more searching, more detailed inquiry into moral and political questions and its interest in the analysis of the mysteries and perturbations of the human mind. To the new age, so often skeptical, tentative, and self-conscious in its exploration of hidden motives, a new style was necessary, a style that could express the mind as it was in movement, could record the thought at the moment it arose. The amplifications and formal figures of Elizabethan rhetoric were as unsuitable for their purposes as the roundness of the Ciceronian period wheeling its way to a long-foreseen conclusion. The new style, by some called anti-Ciceronian, appears in new forms which suddenly become important in the new century and remain important for the greater part of the century: for example, the essay and the character. Perhaps I may add also the paradox, which now became so important that one hesitates whether to call it a figure or a form. The first year of the century saw the publication of one of the greatest of English poems that are built upon paradox: I mean *The Phoenix and Turtle,* a poem which suggests that if Shakespeare at the end of the century had turned from dramatic verse to nondramatic he might have been the greatest of metaphysical poets. The paradox appealed to the century because it gave opportunity for antithetical wit and for those surprises of thought which were so valued at the time. It appealed to writers of "strong lines" because, as one writer observed, it is "a Quodlibet, or strain of wit and invention screwed above the vulgar conceit, to beget admiration." In the sense that it was "a strange or admirable opinion held against the common conceit" it appealed to an age with a strong infusion of stoicism. And a dogmatist like Hobbes could defend it as "an opinion not yet generally received," obviously implying that if it was not yet received it soon would be.

In calling the essay a new form I am aware that there are parallels in antiquity, yet Montaigne not without help from Plutarch and Seneca created a new form; and Bacon, who borrowed the word "essay" from Montaigne, followed by Cornwallis, Cowley, and others, created a new form for Englishmen. And in calling the character a new form I am aware that Theophrastus in the fourth century before Christ wrote an influential collection of characters and that to write a character or *descriptio* was for centuries a popular exercise in rhetoric. But in seventeenth-century England it became a new form by reason of the style which was stamped upon it. The quite extraordinary vogue for collections of characters shows that the character which is a witty analysis of a social type was one which the century could not do without. Richard Flecknoe calls it an epigram in prose and distinguishes it from the essay because it does not discourse but gives "only the heads of things in general." With some help from Ben Jonson the style of the character was first fixed in the collection of 1614 which goes under the name of Sir Thomas Overbury. A book written by a schoolmaster, Ralph Johnson, and published in 1665 instructs schoolboys and undergraduates how to write a character. (You may also inquire within on how to make colloquies, essays, epigrams, fables, epistles, hymns, acrostics, epitaphs, and epithalamia, also for the "Rules for moving the Passions.") First, he defines the character as "a witty and facetious description of the nature and qualities of some person, or sort of people." Then he gives

Rules for making it.

1. Chuse a Subject, *viz.* such a sort of men as will admit of variety of observation, such be, drunkards, usurers, lyars, taylors, excise-men, travellers, pedlars, merchants, tapsters, lawyers, an upstart gentleman, a young Justice, a Constable, an Alderman, and the like.

2. Express their natures, qualities, conditions, practices, tools, desires, aims, or ends, by witty Allegories, or Allusions, to things or terms in nature, or art, of like nature and resemblance, still striving for wit and pleasantness, together with tart nipping jerks about their vices or miscarriages.

3. Conclude with some witty and neat passage, leaving them to the effect of their follies or studies.

"Witty and facetious," "tart nipping jerks," "Conclude with some witty and neat passage," these are some of the characteristics of a form into which matter can be packed and language be spare and precise, in which paradox and turns of unexpected wit are encouraged, in which a self-conscious and a rather urban society can examine itself with wit and satire. And so the character emerges in a new shape and a new style about the same time as the essay and the epistle.

By general consent the master of the form is John Earle. When his *Microcosmography* was published in 1628, he was twenty-seven years of age, and a fellow of Merton College,

Oxford. His collection has a university flavor as Overbury's has a court flavor: there are characters of an old college butler, a downright scholar, a young gentleman of the university, a university don, a plodding student. But he is far from resembling his own downright scholar of whom he says: "his mind is too much taken up with his mind, and his thoughts not loaden with any carriage besides." Shrewdly observant of the foibles of human nature, he draws a picture of the little world of man, a microcosmography, "a piece of the world discovered," that surprises both by its wit and its perception. The form he is using is mainly for comedy and satire: the analysis of man's function in society, the ridiculing of what departs from the norm. But Earle's norm or touchstone is not fashion or worldly civility or manners for their own sake. Sometimes he gets clean away from society as a point of reference, and there comes into his work a hint of spiritual insight and a beauty rare in this kind of writing. So it is with his character of "A Child." There is still wit and unexpectedness, but instead of "tart nipping jerks" a sense of grace in childhood found also in *The Winter's Tale* and in Vaughan and Traherne.

What has also established the supremacy of Earle is the perfection of his form. We read him with expectation because we can never forecast the thought that he will give us or the delicacy with which he will clothe it. Take this sentence on "A Pot-Poet": "He drops away at last in some obscure painted cloth, to which himself made the verses, and his life, like a can too full, spills upon the bench." The placing of the verb "spills" shows him a master of cadence, and the simile fits like a glove. Here is a writer who uses wit not because he is clever (though he is) but because he is wise, not to dazzle but to illuminate. And as for cliché he seems incapable of it; he even eschews proverb. Look in a modern dictionary of proverbs—a branch of lexicography in which the seventeenth century excels—and you find this saying quoted from *The Fortunes of Nigel:* "Three things are thrown away in a bowling-green, namely, time, money and oaths." But the saying is not proverbial. Scott had been reading Earle and remembered the opening of his character of "A Bowl-Alley." Like everything Earle wrote, it was minted in his brain.

He kept strictly to his form. It is, of course, very limited, and Earle's is only a minor classic. No one could use it today without being consciously archaic. As the century advances it tends to turn into something else, perhaps into the essay or into exhortation as in Fuller's *Holy and Profane State.* One of the best characters of the century is Halifax's *Character of a Trimmer* (1688), but it is not a character in the Overburian sense or the Overburian style.

> Our *Trimmer* is far from Idolatry in other things, in one thing only he cometh near it, his Country is in some degree his Idol; he doth not Worship the Sun, because 'tis not peculiar to us, it rambles about the World, and is less kind to us than others; but for the Earth of *England,* tho' perhaps inferiour to that of many places abroad, to him there is Divinity in it, and he would rather dye, than see a spire of *English* Grass trampled down by a foreign Trespasser.

Halifax's "character" turns out to be a brilliant political essay to be read by any man today who refuses to believe that political truth is the prerogative of one party and conceives there may be some virtue in trimming the ship of state.

Another writer who found the character too confined and turned it into something else is Samuel Butler. He had made his name as the author of *Hudibras* before he turned to the character, perhaps in the last years of his life (he died in 1680), but the form was too narrow for so robust a writer. In such a character as that of "A Small Poet" he draws away from the old pithy conceited way of writing to a more fluent, more vigorous form, and is on the way to writing a satirical essay. With him we are getting into the age of common sense and reason, of knowing what's what. His prose moves easily and sturdily with sentences that have no predestined shape except that dictated by the sense. Metaphors have almost disappeared and are replaced by similes striking and homely, such as "When he [the small poet] writes he commonly steers the sense of his lines by the rhyme that is at the end of them, as butchers do calves by the tail." In short, we are a step or two nearer to Jonathan Swift, the Swift of *A Tale of a Tub,* a seventeenth-century book though not published till 1704.

Much of Butler's essay is ridicule of Edward Benlowes, a metaphysical poet of the most difficult and rugged kind, a writer of "strong lines" and dark conceits, as much a writer of private verse for initiates as Butler was of public verse and prose which all may read. If Butler used conceits it was only in *Hudibras* for satirical and burlesque purposes. In conversation with John Aubrey and in his character of "A Quibbler" he distinguished between two sorts of quibbling. First, quibbling with words, the figures of words to which the Elizabethans had been much addicted, a sort already cried down. The second sort, quibbling with sense, he complained, still prevailed. But he foresaw that the days when it could be used seriously were numbered. And when quibbling with sense went out, the character after the manner of Overbury and Earle was doomed. Moreover, other ways of examining in prose the conduct of men and women in and out of society were becoming available. The early seventeenth century saw the beginning of periodical journalism, the late seventeenth century saw the rise of the literary periodical and the periodical essay, and in the early eighteenth century Steele and Addison were to reach a wider public than any character writer of the seventeenth century. A little later, after much groping, another form emerged, a form of which the use and popularity are not yet exhausted after more than two centuries of constant practice, the form of the novel.

In this form alone is the seventeenth century disappointingly meager. In his book on the English novel George Saintsbury has a chapter on what he calls the four wheels of the novel wain in the eighteenth century: Richardson, Fielding, Smollett, Sterne. Apply this metaphor to the sixteenth century and we may say that the four wheels of the Elizabethan novel wain are Lyly, Sidney, Nashe, and Deloney. Among them they attempted nearly all the kinds of prose fiction known to the sixteenth century. From our modern point of view Lyly's *Euphues* is more a treatise on education than a novel of contemporary manners, for the narrative interest in Lyly is swamped, as it is not in Gascoigne's earlier *Adventures of Master F. J.*, by the writer's addiction to morals, and by the way in which he detains his subject by rhetorical amplification and all the figures of vocal ornament. But what seem vices to our age were virtues to Lyly's, and his novel was for a few years a resounding success. Nashe in *The Un-*

fortunate Traveller gave his age an English example of a picaresque novel, almost a solitary example; and Deloney provided some of the very few examples of novels of trade life. As for the *Arcadia* it is superficially a pastoral-chivalric romance, but in effect it is a romantic epic like *The Faerie Queene* which is set in Arcadia but is nourished by deeply felt reflections upon politics, religion, and the passions of men and women. There is much in the *Arcadia* that is alien to the modern conception of the novel, yet if we were to accept the qualities which a modern critic, Edward Sackville-West, looks for in the novel of today, in what respects does the *Arcadia* fall short? He demands of the novel that its style be conscious, that the chief persons display intelligence or sensibility or both, that the story show judgment and imagination no matter what kind of experience it may deal with, that the dialogue proceed on a level above that of everyday life, that the plot be significant, and the whole aim at and achieve the effect of poetry.

Now it could be maintained that the late sixteenth century made a promising start in the novel form; yet of the four writers I have mentioned two only were much read in the seventeenth century, the aristocrat and the tradesman, Sidney and Deloney. While Deloney's novels were still leading a subterranean existence in chapbook form among the semi-literate in the time of Johnson, the *Arcadia* alone continued to be polite reading; it survived to leave its mark upon the fiction of Samuel Richardson. What is more remarkable is that the Elizabethans seem to have had no, or insignificant, successors. The best minds of the seventeenth century, a century than which there is no richer in English literature, did not interest themselves in fiction, could not conceive that it might be taken seriously. If we disqualify Bunyan's allegorical narratives, as I think we should, we have to say that the century did not add a single piece of any considerable merit to the roll of English fiction. Look abroad and we find that one of the world's great masterpieces belongs to the earliest years of the century. *Don Quixote* has had as much effect upon English novelists as any other foreign novel, but the disciples of Cervantes are not men of the seventeenth century. They are Fielding, Sterne, and Smollett. So long have we to wait for the novel to take root in English soil.

It is pitiful to read the histories of the novel and observe how hard put to it the historians are to fill the gap between Sidney and Defoe, how they are compelled to scrape the bottom of the seventeenth-century barrel. True, there is the romance, which owes something to the *Arcadia* and more to France. There is a resolve of Charles Lamb's which any scholar will do well to remember and if possible to act upon. It is this: "what any man can write, surely I may read." But I have yet to meet the reader who has convinced me that he has really read through, much less enjoyed, any considerable number of seventeenth-century romances, whether native or translated from the French. They were read in their time, of course. A father complained of his daughters that instead of applying themselves to their Catechism and *The Lady's Calling* they filled their heads with speeches from romances. The consequence was that when they met their brother's tutor at Oxford and heard nothing in his talk about Love and Honour (the main themes of these romances) they fell into downright scolding at him and said that if this was your Oxford breeding they had rather their brother went to Constantinople to learn manners. There is a better-known and better example. The fantastic situations and sentiments in Roger Boyle's *Parthenissa* did not prevent Dorothy Osborne from reading it and relating the conduct of the characters to the standards and values of real life, or from writing what is one of the earliest, as it is one of the liveliest, critiques of an English work of fiction.

It was long before the word "novel" acquired its present meaning. It first appears in the sixteenth century and then as an English version of *novella,* and in the late seventeenth century it was applied to short works of romantic fiction like Mrs. Behn's or Mrs. Manley's or like Congreve's *Incognita.* Still to Johnson the novel was "a small tale, generally of love," and to Chesterfield it was "a little gallant history, which must contain a great deal of love, and not exceed one or two small volumes. . . . A Novel is a kind of abbreviation of a Romance; for a Romance generally consists of twelve volumes, all filled with insipid love nonsense, and most incredible adventures." But Richardson and Fielding, while they wrote what we shall agree to call novels in our sense of the word, did not call them novels. They called them histories: *The History of Clarissa, The History of Tom Jones.* By so calling them they dissociated their work from the romance and from the abbreviated romance or novel. For the romance meant to them as to Johnson a tale of wild adventure in war and love, whereas Richardson and Fielding are historians of human character and manners. They keep within the limits not merely of possibility but of probability.

It is no doubt beyond the wit of any man to say why the

novel should have been born in the eighteenth century and not earlier, but it is not so difficult to see how the seventeenth century prepared the way for Defoe and Richardson. The increase in population and in the reading public, the coming of age of the middle classes, the appearance and rapid growth of periodical journalism, the breakdown of the old system of private patronage and the determination of the new patrons—the publishers and the booksellers—to give a new public what it wanted, whether in periodical journalism or in other forms—these play their part. So do more abstruse reasons which have been best stated by Professor Ian Watt in his admirable book, *The Rise of the Novel* (1957). He points to the parallel manifestation in philosophy, especially in Descartes and Locke, where truth is made to depend upon individual experience, not upon collective tradition. And I would point to a parallel manifestation in biography. More and more biography becomes the art of showing exactly how a man differs from the rest of mankind and the better to show this it presents, in Mr. Watt's words about the novel, "particular individuals having particular experiences at particular times and at particular places." For whatever reasons, it became possible in the early eighteenth century to write works of fiction not merely about high life as in the romances about kings and queens, princes and princesses, and their impossible adventures and passions, and not merely —this is almost as important—about low life, as in the despicable examples of seventeenth-century picaresque fiction, but about men and women of a middle station in life, men and women—I was going to say—like you and like me.

It is paradoxical but I think true that what Defoe's novels owe to the seventeenth century, in which he lived more than half his life, they do not owe to its fiction. The notion that a work like *Moll Flanders* derives from the seventeenth-century dregs of picaresque fiction has been abandoned. It is quite different. It is not vulgar, debased, facetious; it is serious and on the surface at any rate morally earnest. For the origins of his fiction we must look to seventeenth-century books of travel, memoirs, history, biographies and autobiographies, not forgetting the spiritual biographies and autobiographies of Nonconformist circles, day-to-day journalism, the reporting of crime, not the invention of it. His fiction, like Richardson's, pretends to be fact. Both go to extraordinary lengths to persuade their readers that what they are reading is as true as history because it is history. For many years the reading of histories was considered more proper than the reading of novels; perhaps it still is. The young Queen Victoria confided in her diary that she was glad when she finished *Eugene Aram,* "for I never feel quite at ease or at home when I am reading a Novel." A man or woman could read any of Richardson's works and many of Defoe's and be at ease, persuade himself he was being improved.

Is it significant that Defoe was a dissenter, that he inherited from the seventeenth-century Puritans an antiauthoritarian spirit that broke with tradition, looked forward to the future as an era of progress, fostered the useful arts and experimental science, and was antagonistic to the ancient aristocratic system of education based upon the classics? Defoe held

that a man was a scholar who had gone through all the
sciences, had passed a course in natural and experimental
philosophy, and had read over, in translation, the works of
the best masters in these studies. "The knowledge of things,
not words, make a scholar," he says, in words that recall
the *Nullius in verba* of the Royal Society. And again he says:
"Knowledge can never be too diffusive, nor too many men
drink at her streams." What a contrast with the views of
Erasmus or Ascham or Mulcaster! Richardson was no Nonconformist, but like Defoe he missed the training of grammar
school and university, and like Defoe he decried the classics.
I might be more tempted to believe that this practical,
prudential, and progressive spirit, as noticeable in Richardson as in Defoe, had something to do with the invention of
the new novel form were it not that hard on Richardson's
heels, so hard that he galled Richardson's kibe, came the
Etonian Fielding. Here is a man who did not pretend that he
was not writing fiction, but in the initial chapters to the
successive books of *Tom Jones* seems, as George Eliot says,
"to bring his arm-chair to the proscenium and chat with us
in all the lusty ease of his fine English." Here is a man with
no prudential morality about him, who praised *Clarissa*
generously, in the recently recovered letter to Richardson,
for its characters and its comic and tragic scenes but failed
to mention the moral lessons in which the book abounds and
which were the author's professed aim in writing it. Here
is a man who worked happily and freely in that tradition of
polite learning which had survived for so many centuries:
Homer and Virgil, Aristophanes and Lucian, Rabelais and
Cervantes, Shakespeare and Molière.

But when I have said all this, I have not explained why the novel as we think of the novel was not born till the eighteenth century. This lecture must end, like *Rasselas,* with a conclusion in which nothing is concluded.

II

Robert Burton

In *The Advancement of Learning* Bacon recommends as a suitable and much-needed subject for scientific investigation a study of the "affections," that is, the passions or desires of men. Just as before we give medicine to the body we must know a man's constitution and diagnose his disease, so in administering medicine to the mind, we must first know the different characters of men's natures and then the diseases and infirmities of men's minds, the perturbations and distempers of the affections. So Bacon argued in 1605. And in 1621 was published the first edition of a famous Jacobean book which is devoted to the anatomy, that is, to the dissection, of one fearful disease of the mind, the disease of melancholy.

The Anatomy of Melancholy purports to be the work of Democritus Junior, and the name of Robert Burton, given in the Conclusion to the first edition, is removed from later editions. Hiding his name, he pretends, allows him more liberty and freedom of speech. This is partly though perhaps not wholly pretense. Burton tells us so much about himself and his family that the secret of authorship remains no secret to any reader of his book. Let us examine for a few minutes how much of his identity he reveals, for by doing so we shall learn much about the man and something about his book.

He begins with a tremendous Preface, "Democritus to the Reader," sixty-four folio pages in the second edition of 1624, seventy-eight in the fifth of 1638. From this we learn that the author is a scholar who for twenty years and more has led a silent sedentary solitary life in the university, *sibi et musis,* penned up for the most part in his study, a mere spectator of other men's fortunes, a man who delights in cosmography (like Richard Hakluyt), but (again like Hakluyt) has never traveled except by map and card. He possesses little and wants nothing. By profession a divine, he has sought preferment but has not found it. He tells us his Christian name in the remark that where others get their knowledge by books he gets his by melancholizing: "Experto crede Roberto," yet both revealing and concealing the name, for "Roberto" is part of the proverb. And his surname he tells us in an open reference to his elder brother William Burton and his description of Leicestershire, published in 1622 a year after the first edition of Robert's book.

So in the Preface. In the text of his book he tells us much more. His father lived at Lindley in Leicestershire, near Oldbury, on the borders of Warwickshire, where (he says) "I have often looked about me with great delight, at the foot of which hill I was born." His elder brother William lived at Falde, a pleasant village next to Hanbury in Staffordshire, an ancient patrimony belonging to his family. Yet while Robert was born of worshipful parents, he had to add: "I am a younger brother. It concerns me not."

His mother, Dorothy Burton, did not die till 1629, so that she lived to read about herself in her son's book. She had a practical knowledge of medicine, like all self-respecting, public-spirited country gentlewomen of her day, before there were any country doctors to speak of. (Roger North's mother was more than a match in experience for a college of physicians.) Says Robert, she had "excellent skill in chirurgery, sore eyes, aches, etc., and such experimental medicines, as all the country where she dwelt can witness, to have done many famous and good cures upon divers poor folks, that were otherwise destitute of help." One long vacation, when he was staying at his father's house, he observed that his mother prescribed as a cure for the ague "a Spider in a nutshell lapped in silk." With all his book learning in his head, a sophisticated young man from the university, he thought this amulet most absurd and ridiculous, in spite of his respect for his mother and her skill; until at length, rambling amongst authors as was his pleasure, he found this very medicine recommended in Dioscorides, approved by Matthiolus, and repeated by Aldrovandus, *cap. de Aranea lib. de insectis.* Then he began to think better of it.

He tells us much about himself as well as about his family. We hear that he went to school at Sutton Coldfield in Warwickshire, and used to think "no slavery in the world like to that of a grammar scholar"; that he became a Student of Christ Church; that his Latin play *Philosophaster* was publicly performed in his college on February 16, 1618. And when he comes to the section on love melancholy, he tells us that he is a bachelor writing merely from hearsay, observation, and his own reading. He has heard that "an Irish sea is not so turbulent and raging as a litigious wife," and that bachelors cry "hahho" for a wife, yet when they are married make their moan: "if this be true now, as some out of experience will inform us, farewell wiving for my part."

We may learn much about Burton's beliefs. An Anglican divine, he attacks on the one hand the papists and especially the Jesuits, and on the other "nice and curious schismatics." He is no Arminian; neither is he a strict Calvinist, for he believes our will is free in respect of us and things contingent; and he approves of King James's Book of Sports, of dancing, masking, mumming, and stage plays, if opportunely and soberly used. Yet he is no fierce disputant, does not care for religious controversy. He is in every way a moderate man, a middle-of-the-road man, even in that *via media,* the Church of England.

His moderation shows itself in smaller matters. In medicine he dissociates himself equally from the Paracelsians who upheld chemical preparatives and from the Galenists who upheld vegetable preparatives and attacked the heretic Paracelsus for doing in physic what Luther did in divinity. In dress his advice is to observe the mean between prodigality of attire and dressing "like an old image in Arras hangings." As for beer, his advice is to drink neither strong beer nor small: "the middling is fittest."

But remembering how he came to believe in his mother's cure for the ague, can we say that he was moderate in credulity? To this I would reply, first, that his was an age that still believed in a divine order in the universe, a universe to which man was linked by many subtle correspondencies and sympathies; an age that believed in the direct intervention of God and the Devil in human affairs. Second, many of the illustrations he gives and the tales he tells he does not

necessarily believe in. For example, he reports the story of
the hermit visited one night by the Devil in the habit of a
young market wench. As the hermit was on the point of
forgetting his vows, "she vanished on a sudden, and the
devils in the air laughed him to scorn." Then he adds:
"Whether this be a true story, or a tale, I will not much
contend: it serves to illustrate this which I have said."

So much, then, and more does Burton reveal of himself
and his character in his book. A secluded Oxford don, a
scholar going about his business in life without pomp or
splendor, younger son of a family of country gentry long
established in the Midlands, we need to know little more
about him for our purposes. In 1621, when the first edition
of his book was published, he was forty-four years old. He
contributed Latin poems to various small volumes of com-
memorative verse which it was then the fashion to publish
in Oxford and Cambridge, volumes like that in which
Lycidas appeared. His satirical Latin play on true and false
learning, *The Philosophaster,* remained in manuscript till
the nineteenth century. He is a man of one book, but that
book is an encyclopedia of Renaissance learning, and there
are few topics—literary, scientific, psychological, spiritual—
which occupied the minds of men in the early seventeenth
century upon which he does not touch.

He died at or very near the time that some years earlier
he had predicted from the calculation of his own nativity.
Both Aubrey and Wood report the gossip that Burton put
an end to his own life rather than there should be a mistake
in the calculation. This is one of those libels upon the dead
to which the memories of famous men are particularly

vulnerable. It is mere gossip, and it would not have been told of Burton if it had not already been told of the famous Italian physician and philosopher, Jerome Cardan, and of the English astrologer Simon Forman.

There is another anecdote about him which may or may not be true, and this too had been told about another before him. He was subject to melancholy—he wrote his book to purge himself of the disease—and when his melancholy fits increased, we are told, nothing could make him laugh but going to the bridge across the Thames near his college "and hearing the ribaldry of the bargemen, which rarely failed to throw him into a violent fit of laughter." If this is true, then Democritus Junior was but following the example of Democritus Senior. For Democritus Senior, who also led a life of studious retirement, would sometimes walk down to the haven at Abdera—Burton tells us this himself—"and laugh heartily at such variety of ridiculous objects which there he saw." Certainly, Burton was not dependent upon the language of Thames bargemen for the remarkable display of vituperative fireworks which blazes especially in the section on Love Melancholy. He had but to read, and he did read, his remarkable collection of ephemeral pamphlets of the sixteenth and early seventeenth centuries, pamphlets about monsters, murders, "accidents by flood and field," crime and punishment, rogues and vagabonds, deceits of tradespeople and women, jestbooks, just the kind of literature which Sir Thomas Bodley dismissed as "baggage literature" and did not care to admit into his library. Fortunately, Burton bequeathed to the Bodleian Library all those books in his very considerable collection which it did not already possess;

and these, many of them in English, are now among that library's rarest treasures. The remainder of his books he left to his college, where they still are. A catalogue of his books in the Bodleian Library and in Christ Church was published by the Oxford Bibliographical Society in 1926 in a number specially devoted to Burton, which contains also essays by Sir William Osler, Edward Bensly, and other good Burtonians on the man, his library, and his book. He died in his college in 1640, having resided there since 1599.

The first edition of the *Anatomy* of 1621 is in quarto; the other seventeenth-century editions—and they are many— are in folio. To each successive edition published in his lifetime he made additions, especially in the second of 1624 and the third of 1628. In his revisions he expunged little, but as he never ceased reading, he added more and more observations in the appropriate places. He found it easier to write more, he tells us, than to alter what he had written. Printers' errors increased with every successive edition, and some remain uncorrected in modern editions.

There is no edition that tells us how his book grew, or what are his sources, acknowledged and unacknowledged, and how he handled them. The task of an editor is indeed formidable. There is the size of the book and the many editions each containing new matter, and there is the remoteness and range of Burton's sources. I have already mentioned a break in cultural tradition in the late seventeenth century and how one of the signs of this break is the way in which the old bibliographical tools were abandoned and supplanted by new ones. Burton wrote before the break, and one of the attractions of the book to a modern reader is that it introduces him to a world of forgotten and recondite learning of the Middle Ages and the Renaissance. For example, if we want to know what a well-read and intelligent man thought of the four humors just before William Harvey published the results of his researches on the circulation of the blood in 1628, or if we want to know what was thought of man's understanding and of will and reason before Hobbes in mid-century and Locke at the end announced their conclusions on the mind of man, we cannot easily do better than consult Burton's digression, near the beginning of his book, on the anatomy of the body and of the three principal faculties of the soul, vegetal, sensible, and rational. But all this forgotten learning, while of great interest to the carefree reader, makes an editor's task formidable. The text bristles with quotations, mostly in Latin; so do the margins,

> In which the Text like Land incircled, floates
> 'Midst the vast Ocean of this Authors Notes.

Some are from classical writers, but by far the greater number are not. Burton quotes from the church Fathers, from the schoolmen, from the medieval encyclopedists, from the mass of humanistic writings in Latin on almost all conceivable subjects, the moralists, geographers, astronomers, astrologers, political and medical writers, satirists, poets, writers of romances, theologians—there is no end to the list. At first glance he might be mistaken for a pedant, but it is soon seen that he is not commanded by his learning, but commands it. He bears no resemblance to Henry Dodwell (d. 1711), for a brief tenure Camden Professor of Ancient History at

Oxford, of whom Macaulay said that "the small intellectual spark which he possessed was put out by the fuel."

Among Burton's English sources are the poems of Chaucer, Spenser, Marlowe, Daniel, Drayton, and Shakespeare: *Venus and Adonis* and *Lucrece* appear mostly in the sections on Love Melancholy, but he refers also to *Romeo and Juliet*. He quotes from more than one play of Jonson's. Usually he cites references to his sources, but not always; and perhaps he is most inclined to omit references to his English sources, as being less authoritative. For example, there is a passage that praises the merits of fishing above those of hawking and hunting, one of the merits being that

> if so bee the angler catch no Fish, yet he hath a wholesome walke to the Brooke side, pleasant shade, by the sweet silver streames; he hath good aire, and sweet smels of fine fresh meadow flowers, hee heares the melodious harmony of Birds, he sees the Swannes, herons, ducks, water-hens, cootes, &c. and many other fowle, with their brood, which hee thinketh better then the noise of hounds, or blast of hornes, and all the sport that they can make.

This is pleasant descriptive prose, and I believe it has been quoted before now as an example of Burton's prose. But it is not his. He took it almost verbatim, perhaps by way of an Elizabethan intermediary, from a *Treatise of Fishing with an Angle* printed by Wynkyn de Worde as early as 1496. Incidentally, this tradition of praising fishing at the expense of hawking, hunting, and fowling has left its mark on the shape and content of *The Compleat Angler*.

What of the structure of the book? The long Preface

"Democritus Junior to the Reader" answers such questions as: Why do I choose the pseudonym Democritus? What structure have I chosen and what style? And why do I, a divine not a physician, write about Melancholy? To this he answers that while the physician cures the soul through the body, and the divine cures the body through the soul, both are needed for a perfect cure. And so his purpose is to anatomize this humor through all the members of our Microcosmus; as great a task, he claims, as to square the circle, to find out the creeks and sounds of the Northeast or Northwest passages, to perfect the motion of Mars and Mercury which so crucifies the astronomers, or to rectify the Gregorian calendar.

In the Preface, for satirical reasons, he interprets melancholy in the widest sense to include any departure from right reason, and shows its prevalence in all countries and among all classes of men. All sorts, sects, ages, and conditions are out of tune, suffering from folly, melancholy, madness, all but one disease. Never were there so many fools and madmen. Consider the variety of religious sects. Consider the horrors of war. Think of the conventions of society by which a poor sheepstealer is hanged who steals to save himself from starving, while a great man in office may safely rob whole provinces. Or think of the evils of the law and the corruptions of judges. Kingdoms, politic bodies, these too suffer from melancholy, for states, like men, may be healthy or sick. For example, what dishonor is it to the English nation that Ireland should lie waste so long or that English cities and country districts should compare so unfavorably with the rich United Provinces of Holland! London excepted,

English towns are mean and poor and full of beggars. Idleness is the *malus genius* of the nation. It is even too lazy to catch its own fish.

Then he indulges himself for a time in the luxury of fashioning his own Utopia, the site maybe *Terra Australis Incognita,* latitude 45°, where there is room enough and perpetual spring. And he fashions a land of twelve or thirteen provinces, each with a metropolis of its own; a country in which the land is public, not private; where there is town planning; where there are few laws but these severely kept; where lawyers, judges, and physicians are restricted in number and paid by the state; where performers of noble exploits, inventors and writers, are rewarded and the aged pensioned; where theft is not punished by death, though murder and adultery are; where no man may marry before he is twenty-five or woman before she is twenty; where usury is tolerated—since, as he says, he is speaking of men, not of gods—but with interest at not more than 8 per cent; and where the nation does not make war unless the cause is very just.

And so the address to the reader concludes with the reflection that all the world is melancholy and dotes: princes and great men, philosophers, scholars—"Much learning hath cracked their sconce"—poets, lovers, women, sailors, there are no exceptions. All are of Gotham parish.

Like the section on love melancholy, the address is in his lightest vein. "If I have been too light and comical for a Divine, 'tis not I but Democritus . . . it is a Cento collected from others, not I, but they that say it. . . . I promise you a more sober discourse in my following treatise." And he keeps his promise. For now in the *Anatomy* proper he dismisses from his attention those who are merely metaphorically mad or lightly mad, those who experience that transitory melancholy from which no man is free, not even a Stoic, and proceeds to his task of anatomizing melancholy through all its parts and species as if it is a habit or disease, a settled humor, not errant but fixed.

There is nothing eccentric in the elaborate division and subdivision of the *Anatomy*. Parallels can be found in many a work of his age. It is an elaborate arrangement, but it is a logical one. Each of the three partitions is divided into sections which are divided into members which are sometimes divided into subsections. I will only say that of the three partitions the first considers the kinds, causes, symptoms, and prognostics of melancholy; the second, the cure of melancholy; and the third is devoted to a detailed examination of two especially important types of melancholy—love melancholy and religious melancholy. Because he proceeded by a logical method, because each of the many facets of his argument is allotted its rightful place, he was able in successive editions to add new evidence without having to rewrite and without spoiling the structure of the whole.

Occasionally and deliberately, he allows himself a digression. Three of these seem to me of special interest. To the digression on the anatomy of the body and the soul I have already referred. Another is on the misery of scholars, and among them those who "in collegiis suis in æternum incarcerati, inglorie delitescant." The reference is 1.2.3.15; that is, subsection 15 of member 3 of section 2 of partition 1. A third digression (at 2.2.3) he calls a digression of the air.

And we shall do well to read this digression if we wish to
know what problems in geographical discovery, natural
history, and astronomy interested a well-read man not specially qualified in scientific research but alive to much of the
intense speculation of the time from Copernicus to Kepler
and Galileo. Logic had brought him to the point where he
was to consider the effect of air and climate upon the constitution, and with some relief he relaxes the close work of
dissection and roams at will in the exciting air of astronomical speculation. More amusing passages may be found
in the sections on love melancholy, more eloquent and moving in the section on religious melancholy, but none gives
a better idea of the alertness of this secluded scholar to any
notion of the mind of man. Burton's attitude is one of ex-
cited and amused skepticism. He is amused at but not convinced by the eccentrics and epicycles which the astronomers had invented "to salve all appearances." They seemed
to him like tinkers who stop one hole and make two. Between them the world was tossed in a blanket, the earth
"hoised" up and down like a ball. Burton is content to say
of these matters—as of what happens to cuckoos and swal-
lows in winter—"as yet we know not." There is no "irritable
reaching after fact," any more than there is in *Paradise
Lost*. The new takes its place beside the old in a rich world
of speculation, but faith is not assailed.

Burton's book has been read for a variety of reasons.
Byron recommended it as "useful to a man who wishes to
acquire a reputation of being well read with the least trou-
ble." Sterne made many unacknowledged pilferings from
it, subtly changing the tone of his borrowings to suit the

Shandean world. And in the days when journalists were permitted to quote Greek and Latin, Thackeray's Captain
Shandon found the book a "wonderful repertory of learning" from which to take quotations. But the devotees of
Burton go to the book for its own sake and for the humanity
it displays on a subject of perennial interest to man. Like
Diogenes and Democritus this solitary man walked abroad
to look into the world, but not as they did, he says, "to scoff
and laugh at all, but with *a mixed passion.*" The phrase is
found more than once. As he watches the behavior of men
and women in love, the spectacle is a tragicomedy moving
him now to satire and comedy and now to write "in a mixed
Tone." The section which is lightest and least mixed in tone
is the second of the three sections on love melancholy, that
on the symptoms of love. Here this heart-whole bachelor
laughs and scoffs at the vanities and fopperies of man and
woman in the spirit of Democritus and Lucian. He craves
leave for a while to re-create himself after his laborious
studies in the first and second partitions and before he ar-
rives at the section on religious melancholy. Here he heaps
up piles of nouns, adjectives, phrases, many of them labori-
ously collected from a thousand love-sick authors and
shrewd satirists; but the assembly and the placing of them
are his own cunning.

> The major part of Lovers are carried headlong like so
> many brute beasts, reason counsells one way, thy
> friends, fortunes, shame, disgrace, danger, and an
> ocean of cares that will certainly follow; yet this furious
> lust præcipitates, counterpoiseth, weighs downe on
> the other: though it be their utter undoing, perpetuall

infamy, losse, yet they will doe it, and become at last
insensati, void of sense; degenerate into doggs, hogges,
asses, brutes; . . . Love is blinde, as the saying is,
Cupid's blinde, and so are all his followers. . . . Every
Lover admires his mistris, though shee be very de-
formed of her selfe, ill favored, wrinkled, pimpled,
pale, red, yellow, tand, tallow-faced, have a swolne
Iuglers platter face, or a thin, leane, chitty face, have
clouds in her face, be crooked, dry, bald, gogle-eied,
bleare-eyed, or with staring eyes, she lookes like a
squis'd cat, holds her head still awry, heavy, dull,
hollow-eyed, black or yellow about the eyes, or squint-
eyed, sparrow mouthed, *Persean* hook nosed, have a
sharpe fox nose, a red nose, *China* flat, great nose, *nare
simo patuloque,* a nose like a promontory, gubber-
tushed, . . . beetle browed, a Witches beard, . . .
lame, splea-footed, *as slender in the middle as a cow
in the wast,* . . . an harsh voice, incondite gesture,
vile gate, a vast virago, or an ugly tit, a slugge, a fat
fustilugs, a trusse, a long leane rawbone, a skeleton,
. . . and to thy judgement lookes like a mard in a
lanthorne, . . . if he love her once, he admires her
for all this, he takes no notice of any such errors, or
imperfections of body or minde: . . . he had rather
have her than any woman in the world. If he were a
king shee alone should be his Queene, his Empresse.
O that he had but the wealth and treasure of both the
Indies to endow her with, a carracke of Diamonds, a
chaine of pearle, a cascanet of Iewels (a paire of calfe-
skinne gloves of foure pence a paire were fitter) . . .
Venus herselfe, *Panthea, Cleopatra, Tarquins Tana-
quil, Herods Mariamne,* or *Mary* of *Burgundy* if she
were alive, would not match her. . . . All the gracious
elogies, Metaphors, Hyperbolicall comparisons of the
best things in the world, the most glorious names,
whatsoever, I say, is pleasant, amiable, sweet, gratefull,
and delitious, are too little for her. . . . Starres,
Sunnes, Moones, Mettals, sweet smelling flowres,
Odours, perfumes, Colours, Gold, Silver, Ivory, Pearles,

Pretious Stones, Snow, painted Birds, Doves, Hony, Sugar, Spice, cannot expresse her, so soft, so tender, so radiant, sweet, so faire is she.

As for his style there is nothing quite like it. *"Stylus virum arguit,* our style bewrays us."* And here we cannot set him down as a man of moderation. The bitterest attack on it he makes himself in the Preface in a mood of humorous self-depreciation, its

faults of barbarisme, *Dorick* dialect, extemporanean stile, tautologies, apish imitation, a rapsodie of rags gathered together from several dung-hils, excrements of authors, toyes and fopperies, confusedly tumbled out, without art, invention, judgement, wit, learning, harsh, raw, rude, phantasticall, absurd, insolent, indiscreet, ill-composed, indigested, vain, scurrile, idle, dull and dry; I confesse all ('tis partly affected) thou canst not think worse of me than I doe of my self.

If he had had his way, he would have written the book in Latin; but so he could not get it printed. The mercenary stationers, he complained, were willing to print any scurril pamphlet in English; "but in Latin they will not deal." A few passages which he did not think meet for vulgar ears he presented in Latin—for example, a passage on the unfitness for their task of many of the clergy in the Church of England; but he writes his book in English professedly because he could not get it printed in Latin. He lost many European readers in his day; but over the centuries he has gained many readers.

Though a learned writer, he writes in a style not remote from spoken English. It suggests a spoken style because

it is, or gives the impression of being, extemporaneous. I
write, he says, "with as small deliberation as I do ordinarily
speak, without all affectation of big words, fustian phrases,
jingling terms, tropes, strong lines . . . which many so
much affect." Burton, though he respects matter more than
words, yet does not affect the strong lines, the style packed
close even to obscurity, preferred by some of his contemporaries. His style is loose and free.

It does, however, vary with the matter in hand, now
serious, now light; now comic, now satirical; now elaborate,
now remiss. His is seldom a numerous prose, for the quotations break up rhythm. Yet there are passages where the
momentum of his passion is not impeded by the quotations,
the accumulation of nouns and adjectives and verbs, the
short-breathed clauses, which he so much affects.

Finally, I turn from his style once more to the contents
of his book. The only extensive quotation I have made is
from the sections on love melancholy, and these are the best-
known parts of the book. But those who go to the *Anatomy*
merely for pleasing quirks of humor and eccentricities miss
its true nature. Charles Lamb, who wrote a parody of Burton, rather encouraged this approach. Humor and entertainment there are in plenty, and these are not to be missed;
but if this were all the work would not have survived its age.
It would have joined the limbo of books known only to a
few scholars, like Timothy Bright's *Treatise of Melancholy*
or the livelier *Passions of the Mind* by Thomas Wright, to
both of which Burton refers.

It is in the mixed tone that Burton excels, those parts
where he laughs at man's vanities and fopperies and weeps

at his agonies and cruelties, sometimes laughing and weeping at one and the same time. For behind his work there moves the spirit of compassion. Pity urges him to write his book, a fellow feeling for the perturbations of man's mind, which are even more grievous than those of the body. Many examples might be cited: the passage (1.4.1) on those who are driven by melancholy to kill themselves in the bitterness of their passion; the attack on enforced marriages (3.2.5.3) or that on religious hypocrites (3.4.1.1). Or again in the section on religious melancholy (3.4.3.2), that where he observes how good men, often zealous and religious men, who have puzzled themselves about questions of grace, free will, perseverance, come to believe that God has forsaken them, that they are not predestinate; and how these innocent men are often driven to despair and so to religious melancholy by indiscreet pastors, thundering ministers, who, being of a rigid disposition themselves, speak of nothing but hell-fire and damnation. "What a cruel tyranny is this," he writes, "so to insult over and terrify men's souls."

But the passage I would choose to quote is the attack (3.1.3.3) on the hypocrisy of the rich man who is charitable in public and miserly and cruel in private. When Johnson was discussing this work with Boswell, he admitted that it was perhaps overloaded with quotation, but, he added, "there is great spirit and great power in what Burton says, when he writes from his own mind." This passage as well as any shows him writing from his own mind. The few quotations do not impede the sweep of his passion, and the cumulative effect is assisted by the recurrence of the words "he cares not" and "ride on," which serve as a kind of refrain.

Like the dogge in the manger, we neither use it our
selves, let others make use of, or enioy it, part with
nothing while we live, for want of disposing our hous-
hold, and setting things in order, set all the world together by the eares after our death. Poore *Lazarus* lies
howling at his gates for a few crummes, he only seekes
chippings, offals, let him roare and howle, famish, and
eat his own flesh, he respects him not. A poore decayed
kinsman of his, sets upon him by the way in all his
jollity, and runnes begging bareheaded by him, con-
juring by those former bondes of friendship, alliance,
consanguinity, &c. unkle, cosen, brother, father, . . .
Shew some pitty for Christs sake, pitty a sick man,
an old man, &c. hee cares not, ride on: pretend sick-
nesse, inevitable losse of limbes, goods, plead sure-
tiship, or shipwrack, fires, common calamities, shew
thy wants and imperfections, . . . Sweare, protest,
take God and all his Angells to witnesse, *quaere
peregrinum,* thou art a counterfeit cranke, a cheater,
he is not touched with it, *pauper ubique jacet,* ride
on, he takes no notice of it. Put up a supplication to
him in the name of a thousand Orphans, an Hospitall,
a Spittle, a Prison as he goes by, they cry out to him
for aid, ride on, *surdo narras,* hee cares not, let them
eat stones, devoure themselves with vermine, rot in
their own dung, he cares not. Shew him a decayed
haven, a bridge, a schoole, a fortification, &c. or some
publike worke, ride on, good your worship, your
honour, for Gods sake, your countries sake, ride on.
But shew him a role, wherein his name shall be regis-
tred in golden letters, and commended to all posterity, his armes set up, with his devises to be seen,
then peradventure he will stay and contribute; or if
thou canst thunder upon him, as Papists doe, with
satisfactory and meritorious works, or perswade him
by this meanes, he shall save his soule out of hell, and
free it from Purgatory (if he be of any religion) then
in all likelihood he will listen and stay; or that he have
no children, no neere kinsman, heire he cares for at

least, or cannot well tell otherwise how or where to bestow his possessions (for carry them with him he cannot) it may be then he will build some Schoole or Hospitall in his life, or be induced to give liberally to pious uses after his death. For I dare boldly say, vaineglory, that opinion of merit, and this enforced necessity, when they know not otherwise how to leave, or what better to doe with them, is the main cause of most of our good workes. I will not urge this to derogate from any mans charitable devotion, or bounty in this kinde, to censure any good worke; no doubt there be many sanctified, heroicall, and worthy-minded men, that in true zeale, and for vertues sake (divine spirits) that out of commiseration and pitty, extend their liberality, and as much as in them lies, doe good to all men, cloath the naked, feed the hungry, comfort the sick and needy, relieve all, forget and forgive injuries, as true charity requires; yet most part there is *simulatum quid,* a deale of hypocrisie in this kinde, much default and defect.

There is Burton weeping with Heraclitus. Two words appear repeatedly in his book: "feral," that is, deadly, fatal, and "crucify." The feral diseases by which man is crucified —it is his main theme. All his learning does not conceal his humanity. It is not surprising that Johnson was a great admirer. He too was a prey to melancholy and suffered more than most from the diseases of the body and the perturbations of the mind. But Burton wrote for the sound as well as the sick, and I will end with this tribute from one of the great physicians of our century, Sir William Osler: "Burton enriched a subject of universal interest with deep human sympathy, in which soil the roots have struck so deep that the book still lives."

III

Biography

Before the later years of the seventeenth century a man had little chance of being commemorated in a biography if he were not in some way distinguished in the state or in the church. The two outstanding English lives of the sixteenth century, most would agree, are William Roper's life of Sir Thomas More and George Cavendish's life of Cardinal Wolsey. Roper and Cavendish had the great advantage of knowing their men personally, intimately. Roper was More's son-in-law, Cavendish Wolsey's gentleman-usher. And Roper in filling his life of More with vivid talk was able to follow the desire of his heart to preserve to posterity the image of his father-in-law as it existed in his own mind. Both biographies are in a sense medieval tragedies: they show the fall of a man from high estate. This no doubt was an additional recommendation, but they were recommended sufficiently to the notice of contemporaries by the eminence of More and Wolsey in church and state. Until the later seventeenth century biography remained the servant of church and state, and the life of a mere man of letters or a mere man of science was thought unworthy of extended notice.

I say "of extended notice," for there were dictionaries of writers which gave a few facts about their lives and lists of their works. One of the most interesting and valuable was compiled by John Bale and printed in 1548 and in an enlarged edition in 1557. It may be argued that bilious Bale (as Fuller called him) distinguished himself more by these works than by the virulence of his Protestant propaganda in play and pamphlet. Dictionaries of English poets and playwrights of this kind were published also in the seventeenth century: the *Theatrum Poetarum* of Milton's nephew Edward Phillips (1675), and in 1691 the admirable *Account of the English Dramatic Poets* by Gerard Langbaine. But these do not give extended notices, and belong more to bibliography than to biography.

Some are still puzzled that it is today impossible to write a biography of Shakespeare that can be more than a list of external events; yet it is not surprising when we remember that the will to write a biography of a mere dramatist and poet did not appear in England until all had died who could have known Shakespeare in the flesh. As late as 1691 the only news of his life that Langbaine passes on to us, apart from the date of his death and particulars of the monument in Stratford Church, is that he "was born at *Stratford* upon *Avon* in *Warwickshire;* and flourished in the Reigns of Queen *Elizabeth,* and *James* the First." No extended notice of him was printed before 1709 in Rowe's edition of the plays. Lives of dramatists and the care to preserve their letters and papers had to wait until biography was used for other purposes than edification, and then it was too late. For any important knowledge we have of Shakespeare we must look not to his life but to his poetry; and in his poetry we are told not of his life but of what he made of life.

To all this there are some apparent exceptions. I will mention three. First, there are the many lives of men and women, sometimes of humble origin, distinguished by their piety and bearing witness in their deaths as in their lives to the faith that sustained them in a wicked world. A sixteenth-century example and a moving one is Philip Stubbes's account of the death of his young wife, *A Crystal Glass for Christian women* (1591). The earliest beginnings of American biography are of this sort, John Norton's life of John Cotton (1658) and Increase Mather's life of Richard Mather (1670). The intention is as predominantly devotional and doctrinal as in the funeral sermons, where the biography is sometimes a mere appendix or "lean-to." But as Samuel Clarke found, that voluminous collector of the lives of pious Calvinists, they were "accepted with the Saints." A second apparent exception is of a very different kind: to his translation of *Orlando Furioso* (1591) John Harington added a life of Ariosto. If he had written a life of Spenser that would indeed have been surprising, but, as he acknowledged, all that he did here was to gather into one compendious treatise three Italian biographies of Ariosto. A third apparent exception is of far greater interest. In 1598, to his edition of Chaucer's works, Thomas Speght prefixed a life. But it may be argued, and not speciously, that this is the exception that proves the rule. By 1598 Chaucer had become a national figure, the father of English poetry, a poet whose fame stirred the hearts of all patriots. His countrymen revered him as the Italians revered Dante, and scholars were already beginning to give him the honor of a commentary. He was not in his day an important man in the state, but by 1598 he had become one.

Among the most famous of the biographies written in the seventeenth century are the five written by Izaak Walton. Four of these are about famous churchmen: Donne, Herbert, Hooker, Sanderson. The fifth is the life of Sir Henry Wotton, statesman, ambassador, wit, poet, man of affairs, and to Walton also a good Christian. All conform to the traditional view that biography is for edification and for the commemoration of men of the church or the state. Accident rather than necessity induced Walton to become a biographer; and as he looked back after writing four of these lives upon the reasons that led him to commence biographer he could not help wondering that a man of his "education and mean abilities" should come to be publicly in print. He began in this way. His friend Sir Henry Wotton asked him to collect some notes that might be of service to Wotton in writing the life of Donne. But Wotton died in 1639 without writing his old friend's life. And so says Walton:

> I became like those men that enter easily into a *Lawsute*, or a *quarrel*, and having begun, cannot make a fair retreat and be quiet, when they desire it.—And really, after such a manner, I became ingag'd into a necessity of writing the *Life* of *Dr. Donne:* Contrary to my first Intentions: And that begot a like necessity of writing the Life of his and my ever-honoured friend, Sir *Henry Wotton*.

Hence Walton's life of Donne appeared in 1640 before the collected edition of Donne's eighty sermons, and his life of

Wotton in 1651 before a collection of Wotton's shorter pieces (*Reliquiae Wottonianae*). The life of Hooker (1665) was taskwork done at the request of the Archbishop of Canterbury, Gilbert Sheldon, to correct the "dangerous mistakes," doctrinal and otherwise, in Bishop Gauden's life. The life of Sanderson (1678), like that of Hooker, was designed to further the aims and interests of the High-Church party and is much concerned with church history. But the life of Herbert (1670) he wrote to please himself. It was, he says,

> *a Free-will-offering*, . . . writ chiefly to please my self: but, yet, not without some respect to posterity; for though he was not a man that the next age can forget; yet, many of his particular acts and vertues might have been neglected, or lost, if I had not collected and presented them to the Imitation of those that shall succeed us: for I humbly conceive writing to be both a safer and truer preserver of mens Vertuous actions, then tradition, especially as 'tis manag'd in this age.

Johnson said that nobody can write the life of a man "but those who have eat and drunk and lived in social intercourse with him." It is a harsh doctrine and not to be pressed. J. H. Monk's life of Richard Bentley (1830) leaps to the mind as a notable exception. Yet it is true that some of the most famous biographies in the English language—Boswell's life of Johnson, Trevelyan's of Macaulay, Lockhart's of Scott—were written by men who knew their subjects intimately. Donne, Wotton, and Sanderson were Walton's intimate friends; Herbert he had seen, but not talked to; Hooker was a man of an earlier generation, and when he died in 1600 Walton was only seven years old. In consequence, the most personal and intimate of the lives are those of Donne, Wotton, and Sanderson. The life of Herbert belongs to the tradition of the lives of the saints, and Herbert is held up to the Restoration clergy as the model of a country parson.

He took pains to make his lives as accurate as possible, and one or two of them were much revised in successive editions, especially the life of Donne. But of course he made mistakes. I have said that he knew Donne personally, but Donne was nearly twenty years older, and Walton was ill acquainted with the facts of his early life. If Wotton had written the life, as he intended to do, we should be more accurately informed about the poet's youth, for Wotton and Donne were contemporaries at Oxford. In any event, Walton's interest was not in Donne the layman but in Donne the churchman, in the vicar of St. Dunstan's in the West where he was one of Donne's parishioners, in the dean of St. Paul's, the great preacher and divine, with Andrewes the great representative of that part of the Church of England to which Walton himself was devoted. In the life of Hooker he is unjust to Hooker's wife: so the researches of Professor Charles Sisson establish. He took his information and his bias from his connection by marriage with the family of George Cranmer, Hooker's favorite pupil at Oxford and uncle of Walton's first wife. According to Walton's account, Hooker, not considering that the children of this world are wiser in their generation than the children of light, was entrapped into a marriage with a shrew who

brought him neither beauty nor portion, and was "drawn
from the tranquillity of that Garden of Piety of Pleasure,
of Peace, and a sweet Conversation [i.e., his college, Corpus
Christi College, Oxford] into the thorny Wilderness of a
busy World; into those corroding cares that attend a married
Priest, and a Country Parsonage [i.e., Drayton Beauchamp,
near Aylesbury]." He tells how George Cranmer and another
old pupil, Edwin Sandys, visited him in the country, found
him tending his little flock of sheep with a copy of the
Odes of Horace in his hand, how he was snatched away
from their company and told to rock the cradle, and how
their welcome from Mrs. Hooker was so cold that the next
morning they were forced to seek a quieter lodging. It
is one of the most entertaining passages in the *Lives*, but
hardly a detail survives the investigations of Professor
Sisson. It is all false except in the impression it gives of
Hooker's character and (possibly) of his wife's attitude to
his old pupils.

The life of Wotton is the most urbane; the life of Herbert
the most perfect. For writing the life of Herbert, Walton
was well supplied. Herbert had been the friend of Donne
and Wotton, and Walton could draw upon a supply of
anecdotes, the memory of his friends, the poems—from
which he quotes freely—and documentary material, especially letters, from which also he quotes freely. He builds
the character up slowly. It is diffused, not compressed. He
is writing biography, not a mere character piece. Of the
admirable use he makes of anecdote this well-known
example is characteristic. He has been speaking of Herbert's
love of music and how this love would cause him twice
a week to walk in from his parsonage at Bemerton to the

cathedral church at Salisbury and after divine service to sing or play his part at a private music meeting.

> In another walk to *Salisbury*, he saw a poor man, with a poorer horse, that was fall'n under his Load; they were both in distress, and needed present help; which Mr. *Herbert* perceiving, put off his Canonical Coat, and help'd the poor man to unload, and after, to load his horse: The poor man blest him for it: and he blest the poor man; and was so like the *good Samaritan,* that he gave him money to refresh both himself and his horse; and told him, *That if he lov'd himself, he should be merciful to his Beast.*—Thus he left the poor man, and at his coming to his musical friends at *Salisbury,* they began to wonder that Mr. *George Herbert* which us'd to be so trim and clean, came into that company so soyl'd and discompos'd; but he told them the occasion: And when one of the company told him, *He had disparag'd himself by so dirty an employment;* his answer was, *That the thought of what he had done, would prove Musick to him at Midnight; and that the omission of it, would have upbraided and made discord in his Conscience, whensoever he should pass by that place; for, if I be bound to pray for all that be in distress, I am sure that I am bound so far as it is in my power to practise what I pray for. And though I do not wish for the like occasion every day, yet let me tell you, I would not willingly pass one day of my life without comforting a sad soul, or shewing mercy; and I praise God for this occasion:* And now let's tune our Instruments.

How cunningly those famous words are placed: "And now let's tune our Instruments"! They suggest that behind the apparent simplicity of Walton's style, behind the humility of it, there lies much art. Walton was, in a phrase of Charles Dickens', "a not particularly over-educated sort of man." (Anthony Wood thought his *Lives* well done "considering the education of the author"!) He had none of the advantages and, of course, none of the disadvantages of that systematic education at grammar school and university which his friends had enjoyed. Apprenticed at an early age to a London sempster, he took up his freedom in the city of London as a draper. Obviously he was no ordinary tradesman, but by reason of his irregular education writing came hard to him. If with Professor John Butt we look at some of his manuscripts, we may see how clumsy and involved his first thoughts often were: also how highly irregular, as compared with that of his friends, was his spelling. It was an effort for him to write, and in a long life—he died in 1683 in his ninetieth year—he did not write much. But he made the effort, and while his effects seem natural and sometimes even naïve, they are as carefully sought as they are surely secured. The six words at the close of the life of Donne provide another notable example. He ends with a rare word, "re-inanimated." The Oxford Dictionary gives only one example, and that from Donne's sermons: "God . . . shall recollect that dust, . . . and then re-inanimate that man." Perhaps Walton had the passage in mind:

> He was earnest and unwearied in the search of knowledge; with which, his vigorous soul is now satisfied, and employed in a continual praise of that God that first breathed it into his active body; that body, which once was a *Temple of the Holy Ghost,* and is now become a small quantity of *Christian dust:* But I shall see it re-inanimated.

The conversations which Walton reports in these *Lives* are invented conversations. The gist of the matter he is remembering or has been told, but he uses speech when a modern biographer, who did not wish to be accused of being a novelist, would feel obliged to use narrative. George Herbert's speech to the Salisbury music party is an example. Walton might have remembered some of the witty sayings of Sir Henry Wotton, but he could not have remembered the conversation of Herbert or Hooker. In the Preface to the life of his close friend Sanderson (1678) he tells us that he has paraphrased and said what he thinks Sanderson would have said upon the same occasions. He is doing what the classical historians did and what the medieval chroniclers and biographers did: inventing set speeches for his characters, inventing in character, of course, but still inventing. So Cavendish "invented" speeches for Wolsey and Holinshed for many a historical character. Indeed, the invention of such speeches was a common exercise in rhetoric. But the rhetorical "dialogismus" is one thing, and the faithful report of a man's words another. It is a sign of the times that Milton in his *History of Britain* (1670) was strongly of opinion that set speeches ought not to be used in a history

> unless known for certain to have bin so spok'n in effect as they are written, nor then, unless worth rehearsal: to invent such, though eloquently, as some Historians have done, is an abuse of posteritie, raising, in them that read, other conceptions of those times and persons then were true.

Bishop Burnet followed a middle way in a life that is very far from being a saint's life, the *Life and Death of Rochester . . . Written by his own Direction on his Death-Bed*

(1680), a work which called for Johnson's comment, "A good *Death*, there is not much *Life*." In reporting Rochester's deathbed repentance Burnet hardly ever uses *oratio recta*, and he warns his reader that he does not pretend to give the very words used, though he has done so where he could remember them.

"Speeches . . . known for certain to have been so spoken in effect as they are written." But the only way to "know for certain"—and not always then—is to have access to notes of the conversation of famous men taken down while fresh in the memory. Not perhaps before the sixteenth century was the interest in the particular and the individual, in what distinguishes a man from all other men, powerful enough in modern Europe to induce men to make faithful collections of the table talk of eminent men, and one of the very earliest is the collection of Martin Luther's table talk, the *Tischreden*, first published in 1566. In England the earliest collections belong to the seventeenth century, and of these two are outstanding. One of them is the report of the conversation of Ben Jonson written down by the Scottish poet William Drummond of Hawthornden when Jonson visited him about the time of Christmas, 1618. Jonson's talk with Drummond over the wine does not tell us the whole truth about Jonson's character, but thanks chiefly to it Jonson is the only poet and dramatist of that age of whom it is possible to write a biography. For lack of a Drummond we can only dimly guess—if, indeed, we are entitled to guess—at Shakespeare's friendships and enmities, his religion, his manners, and his estimate of contemporary writers.

The other collection is Selden's *Table-Talk,* assembled by his secretary, Richard Milward, over a period of twenty years until a year or so before Selden's death in 1654. Selden was a man of immense and miscellaneous erudition, but he was also a man who had a natural gift for plain speech and homely illustration. A liberal in politics, a skeptic and clergy hater in religion, of him it has been said that "the only thing about which he seems to have had no doubt was the liberty to doubt." Very characteristic of him is this example:

> The reason of a Thing is not to be enquired after, till you are sure the Thing it self be so. We commonly are at *What's the Reason of it?* before we are sure of the Thing. 'Twas an excellent Question of my Lady *Cotten* when Sir Robert Cotten was magnifying of a Shoe, which was *Moses*'s or *Noah*'s, and wondring at the strange Shape and Fashion of it: *But Mr.* Cotten, says she, *are you sure it is a Shooe?*

Collections of table talk are allied to biography and of great service to biographers, yet they are not biography. The same observation may be made of the short historical characters in the number and excellence of which this century excels all others. History was beginning to raise itself above the level of a chronicle, and the new historians profited much in the art of presenting character from Plutarch, Tacitus, and other classical models. The great masters of this kind of portraiture—Halifax, Burnet, above all Clarendon—thought of history and especially the history of their own times as the struggle of personalities, and to this we owe the brilliance of Clarendon's characters of

Hampden, Falkland, Cromwell, or Halifax's of Charles II, and many another. Our posterity may be thought fortunate if it is bequeathed characters as good as these of the leading figures of our troubled times.

But I must return now to biography proper, or rather to the statement I made earlier that before the later years of the century biography was the servant of church and state, and the life of a mere man of letters or man of science was thought unworthy of extended notice. When Thomas Sprat published a life of the poet Cowley in 1668 he felt it necessary to defend himself from the charge of spending too many words on a private man and a scholar. Yet about this very time there were two men busily engaged in collecting all that they could come by about any Oxford man who had once put pen to paper. I refer to John Aubrey and his *Brief Lives* and to Anthony Wood. Wood's *Athenae Oxonienses* was published in the same year (1691) as Langbaine's *Account of the English Dramatic Poets,* and while the bibliographical detail is of much the same extent in both, Wood's biographical detail is immensely fuller. He tried to recover all that was recoverable about every one of his authors, however minor. Much of his detail he borrowed from the notes which Aubrey put at his disposal, a generous action for which Aubrey received inadequate thanks.

Aubrey did not write biography, but rather biographical notes which he set down "tumultuarily as if tumbled out of a sack." He was shiftless, "trapish," and perpetually in debt. But he was a man of insatiable curiosity in men, manners, and antiquities. He had noticed that many memorable things had for want of registering been drowned in oblivion, and for that reason—whether he was describing the ancient ruins of Stonehenge and Avebury, or the topography of his own county of Wiltshire, or Hobbes, or Milton—he determined to be minute. His genius drove him on to a task of which few in his age saw the value:

> This searching after Antiquities is a wearisome task.
> . . . methinks I am carried on with a kind of divine Œstrum: for nobody els hereabout hardly cares for it, but rather makes a scorn of it. But methinkes it shewes a kind of gratitude and good nature to revise the memories and memorialls of the pious and charitable Benefactors since dead and gone.

In his *Gentilism and Judaism* he showed an equal zeal in recording the traces of folk customs and beliefs many of which were killed by the Puritan interregnum; for "wars do not only extinguish religion and laws, but superstition, and no suffimen is a greater fugator of phantasms than gunpowder."

He was credulous, and as he derived so much of his information from talk he set down much that was wrong. But he never himself perverted the facts. Why should he? He had no axe to grind, he was gentle, unselfish, and open-hearted, and he had the wit to do something that was worth doing and to do it supremely well. Sometimes he cites his authority with all the scrupulosity of a modern historian. For example, when John Denham was a young student at the inns of court,

> a frolick came into his head, to gett a playsterer's brush and a pott of inke, and blott out all the signes

between Temple-barre and Charing-crosse, which
made a strange confusion the next day. . . . This I
had from R. Estcott, esq., that carried the inke-pott.

What has attracted many a reader not addicted to antiquities to read in John Aubrey is his eye for bright,
significant detail and his gift for sharp, singular phrasing.
"If ever I had been good for anything," he writes, " 'twould
have been a painter. I could fancy a thing so strongly, and
have so clear an idea of it." For example, how vivid is
what he tells us about the eyes of his characters: Ben
Jonson with "one eye lower than t'other, and bigger, like
Clun the player: perhaps he begot Clun"; Milton's eye
dark-gray; Selden's full, gray, and popping; Hobbes's hazel,
with a bright live coal shining within it; Denham's a kind
of light goose-gray, not big, but it had a strange piercing-
ness, not as to shining and glory, but (like a Momus) when
he conversed with you he looked into your very thoughts;
Bacon's a delicate lively hazel eye, said by William Harvey
to be like the eye of a viper; and the eyes of Ralph Kettell,
president of Aubrey's own college (Trinity, Oxford), sharp
and gray, which helped to make his aspect terrible and so
keep down the *juvenilis impetus!*

I have mentioned Sprat's life of Cowley as one of the
earliest that we have of a private person, but that historical
interest is the only interest it has. It belongs to a type of
biography which Johnson despised. It is panegyric: that
is one fault. It is general panegyric: that is another.
Biography is becoming the art of showing precisely how
one man differed from the rest of mankind, and that cannot
be done by panegyric, still less by general panegyric. Minute

matters must be chosen, maintained Johnson, though chosen with discretion. A little earlier than Sprat's *Cowley* came the life that John Davies wrote about his friend the Cambridge poet and scholar, John Hall, a young man of extraordinary parts: "no man," said Hobbes, "had ever done so great things at his age." Davies' *Life* (1657) is not so well known as Sprat's because Hall is not so well known as Cowley, but like Sprat's it is of a private person, and unlike Sprat's it is not merely panegyric: it mentions Hall's carelessness about his personal appearance—he looked on a barber as a tedious torment—his intemperance, his loose talk about religion, and it includes some minute detail, though whether it is discreet you must judge from this example. Hall disliked exercise that required any violent motion of the body, and being inclined to "pursiness and fatness" he cured his obesity "by frequent swallowing-down of pebble stones." This was effectual. Tickell's *Addison* (1721) on the other hand is as much general panegyric as Sprat's *Cowley* and was condemned by Johnson in the words: "I know not well what advantage posterity can receive from the only circumstance by which Tickell has distinguished Addison from the rest of mankind, *the irregularity of his pulse*." Tickell made two mistakes: he gave only one particular, and it was not characteristic. The irregularity of Addison's pulse sets up no train of associations, for it is at variance with all that we know of Addison's moral or intellectual character. Coleridge's devious walk from one side of the footpath to the other can be related, as Hazlitt related it, to his instability of purpose, but Addison, of all persons, should have had a normal pulse.

Let me take two examples of biography written about the turn of the seventeenth century which are not panegyric and which aim at truth through the particular. My first example is from a book little known and little read today: the *Life of Seth Ward Bishop of Salisbury,* written by Walter Pope, Gresham Professor of Astronomy, and published in 1697. This life is separated by less than twenty years from the life which Walton wrote of Sanderson. Both are lives of bishops of the Church of England. Yet the contrast could not be greater. The one is consistently pious and laudatory in tone, the other often secular and even vulgar, and full of detail sometimes but not always illuminating and edifying. The difference is due in some degree not to the spirit of the age but to the difference between Walton and Pope and even to the difference between Sanderson and Seth Ward. But still Walton's *Life* is of a kind that was to become old-fashioned, and for better or worse Pope's was biography of the new kind, though not a very good example of it.

I can best indicate the tone of Pope's life of Seth Ward by quoting what an enemy said about it:

Pray be pleased to recollect, that a Writer of such an History should endeavour at a concise, easie decent Stile, expressing a Reverence for the Memory of the Person whose Life he describes. The Relations ought to be contrived for instruction, and chiefly set as Paterns of Imitation. *Minute* matters ought to be chosen with Discretion, and *common* Passages just toucht and *hinted* at. Whereas your Narration is drest up in a Comical and Bantering Stile, full of dry Scraps of Latin, Puns, Proverbs, sensless Digressions, long

> tedious unedifying Tales, and not without an insipid *Bawdy* Jest . . . I protest I cannot see one instructing Page in the whole History. . . . With a great deal of *Solemnity* you positively affirm that Dr. *Barrow* made use of a Tinder-Box, and had no Buttons upon his Collar; . . . the Biographers ought to set down the *chief* Vertues and Vices of those they represent.

Swift too would have thought Pope's life of Ward vulgar in style and treatment, and so it is. Yet this vulgar life preserves details which throw light from time to time on character or manners. Even the jests are sometimes vivid. Dr. Thomas Weeks, dean of St. Burian in Cornwall, "had Wit enough, but it was not in a wise man's keeping." (Pope might have made the same remark about himself.) When Charles I visited Cornwall, the dean joined the royal party as they were riding in the country and

> being well mounted, and near his Majesty, the King spoke thus to him, *"Doctor you have a pretty Nag under you, I pray how Old is he?"* To which he, out of the abundance of the Quibbles of his heart, return'd this Answer; *"If it please your Majesty, he is now in the Second Year of his Reign."* . . . The good King did not like this unmannerly Jest, and gave him such an Answer as he deserv'd, which was this; *Go, you are a Fool.*

But Charles II would have laughed.

One more example of how a vulgar life may preserve detail that is illuminating. Pope is writing about the scientist Lawrence Rooke, eminent at Wadham College in the "philosophical meeting" there and later to be one of the original members of the Royal Society.

> I never knew him affirm any thing positively, that was dubious. I have said to him, Mr. *Rooke*, I have found out the reason for such a Fenomenon, and given him my Arguments for it, which when he had heard, he has often replied in this manner; And why may it not as well be thus, bringing his reasons for another Hypothesis. Lord, said I then to him, now you confound me, pray tell me what is your Opinion? To which his usual Answer was, *I have no Opinion.*

There is the modern man of science, the "sceptical chemist." It reminds one of Sir William Petty's remark that the Royal Society should not have chosen St. Andrew for its patron saint, but rather St. Thomas, for he would not believe until he had seen. I said earlier what a contrast between Walton's life of Sanderson and Pope's life of Ward. What a contrast, let me add, between Lawrence Rooke and Sir Thomas Browne, Browne never backward in hazarding an opinion on any problem presented to him and Rooke affirming nothing positively that was dubious. They seem to be living in different ages, yet they were exact contemporaries.

If we look for the best example before Johnson of biography that is not general panegyric and that aims at truth through the particular we shall find it in Roger North's lives of his three brothers, written just after the turn of the century. Two of these brothers were men of some fame: Francis, Lord Keeper Guilford, who became Lord Chancellor under Charles II, and Dudley who after making a fortune in Turkey and the Near East was employed by the Crown to reform two government departments, the Customs and the Treasury. The third, John, was a scholar who rose to become master of Trinity, Cambridge. Roger wrote to defend their memories, so that he is to some extent a partial biographer; but he sees his brothers' faults as well as their virtues. Though he writes family biography, he does not write general panegyric. But hear his own words on the function of a biographer:

> A Life should be a Picture; which cannot be good, if the peculiar Features, whereby the Subject is distinguish'd from all others, are left out. Nay, Scars and Blemishes, as well as Beauties, ought to be expressed; otherwise, it is but an Outline fill'd up with Lillies and Roses.

And put beside that a statement prefixed by the painter Jonathan Richardson before his life of Milton. Though published in 1734 it was already the fifth extended life of Milton to be written.

> If I can give a more Exact, and a more Just Idea of *Milton,* and of *Paradise Lost* than the Publick has yet had of Either, I am Assur'd it will be Acceptable to all Honest and Ingenuous Minds of What Party Soever. This is All I Intend; not a Panegyrick, not to give my Own Sense of What a Man should be, but what This Man Really was.

Readers of the lives of Francis and Dudley North who are not interested in matters of church and state and the legal profession in the later Stuart period may have to do a certain amount of skipping; but the lives give many vivid glimpses of life and manners in seventeenth-century England. In the life of John North there is nothing about politics, for he led the private life of a scholar in the sheltered world of academic Cambridge. Roger writes of him with affection but with an affection that does not conceal his brother's infirmities. For example:

> The Doctor's greatest, or rather only, Infirmity was a natural Timidity, owing to a feeble Constitution of Body, inclining to the effeminate. . . . One would have expected that a Youth at the University, no Freshman, nor mean Scholar, should have got the better of being afraid in the dark; but it was not so with him, for when he was in Bed alone, he durst not trust his Countenance above the Cloaths. For some time he lay with his Tutor, who once, coming home, found the Scholar in Bed with only his Crown visible. The Tutor, indiscretely enough, pulled him by the Hair; whereupon the Scholar sunk down, and the Tutor followed, and at last, with a great Outcry, the Scholar sprung up, expecting to see an enorm Spectre.

The century has prepared the way for Johnson and for Boswell, whose *Life of Johnson* is of all the biographies in the world the one that makes the most splendid use of table talk. Scars and blemishes as well as beauties, the truth for better or worse, the aim to distinguish one man from all others and the better to do so to exhibit his private conduct, these are the very principles of Johnson and of Boswell.

IV

Sir Thomas Browne

To begin with, I take a text from the third chapter of *Urn Burial,* and in the manner of some seventeenth-century preachers I squeeze and wring my text for the meaning I find in it. Browne is discussing the ways in which men of old disposed of their dead:

> To burn the bones of the King of Edom for Lyme seems no irrational ferity; But to drink of the ashes of dead relations, a passionate prodigality.

He is a remarkable writer who can so use his native language that even a couple of short sentences cannot possibly be mistaken for another's. Yet that is what Browne has done here, what he does in almost any other sentences we care to choose. If challenged to say why this short passage is characteristic, I should point to these qualities:

1) A very subtle ear for the values of vowel and consonant sound. That reveals itself in the variety of vowel sound in the opening phrase—"To burn the bones of the King of Edom for lime"—and in its murmuration of *n*'s and *m*'s. Alliteration is here: "To burn the bones," "to drink of the ashes of dead relations," "a passionate prodigality," but

it is not the mechanical alliteration of a euphuist who uses it for balance and sound. It is used here as an intensive of matter and feeling.

2) There is care for musical phrasing and cadence. There is balance, but again not the mechanical balance of the euphuists. If we examine the rhythms at the end of each sentence, we find in "[ir]rational ferity" two dactyls, and in "passionate prodigality" a trochee inserted between two dactyls. There is balance, but there is variety. There is sameness, but there is difference. Similarly, we notice the ellipsis of the verb in the second sentence; a euphuist would not have omitted a balancing verb. There is asymmetry, then, but there is symmetry enough to make the asymmetry felt.

3) This is the prose of a man as much at home in Latin as in English, amphibious prose, or since I am speaking of Browne let me call it utraquistic prose. Emerson, a great admirer of Browne, observes how these two elements in the language are combined in every great style. "The children and labourers use the Saxon unmixed. The Latin unmixed is abandoned to the colleges and Parliament." But no sentence is "made of Roman words alone, without loss of strength." In these two sentences of Browne's the Latin words are reserved for the ends of the sentences. The action is in "Saxon"—"to burn the bones of the King of Edom," "to drink of the ashes"; the moral judgment is in Latin—"no irrational ferity," "a passionate prodigality." These latinisms are not dead and abstract. Their meaning is exact, and they have behind them the pressure of moral fervor.

4) This is a close-packed style, "strong-lined" as the seventeenth century would have called it. The Latin makes for compression; and observe once more the omission of the verb. Sir Kenelm Digby who annotated the *Religio Medici* tells Browne in a letter that his work is "so strongly penned, as requireth much time and sharp intention but to comprehend it." The sentences we have here are meditations, *Pensées*, far removed from a Ciceronian roundness.

5) Lastly, to use so short a passage to illustrate the author's thought and outlook would be fantastic, yet we may notice the out-of-the-way learning, the strikingly unexpected nature of the thought, and the concern with mortality. Above all, we may notice that thought and expression are one and indivisible. As the thought rises to the mind, so and with the same act of the imagination rises the "sense of musical delight, with the power of producing it."

What manner of man was it who wrote these sentences? The work we go to, above all, if we wish to know that, is the *Religio Medici*. It is one of the most personal books written since Montaigne, nothing but "a memorial unto me," he says. But his egotism is without offense, for he writes not for self-glory but to express his faith. When he wrote the book he lacked the use of a good library. What to Browne seemed a handicap is to us, perhaps, an advantage. It has been said that a scholar ought to write his best book when his library has been burnt to the ground. Browne without a library wrote not perhaps his best book, but his simplest.

It was circulated in manuscript before it was printed, in a pirated and imperfect text, in 1642; then in a better text

and with the author's blessing in 1643. In that year Browne
was thirty-eight years old. He had been to Winchester
and Oxford—Broadgates Hall, which became Pembroke
College while Browne was up—had studied at Montpellier
and Padua, and in 1633 had proceeded doctor of medicine
at Leyden. For some years he practiced as a physician at
Halifax in Yorkshire, and there he wrote the *Religio Medici*.
In 1637 he was persuaded by friends to move to Norwich,
then disputing with Bristol the distinction of being the
second largest town in the British Isles, and there he
remained as a respected physician and learned antiquary
and man of science for the rest of his outwardly uneventful
life. He seems hardly to have left the neighborhood of
Norwich. He married in 1641 and had several children one
of whom became a sailor and another a London physician
with a fashionable practice. He did not conceal his
Royalist sympathies, but he remained a passive Royalist
during the civil wars, content to perform his duties as
physician and happy in the companionship of his family
and friends, his books and his scientific work, rejoicing
heartily when the Stuart dynasty was restored. He died in
1682. That he died on his birthday is a coincidence in
which he would have delighted. But he would not have
called it a coincidence.

In the *Religio Medici* he writes: "Now for my life it is
a miracle of thirty years, which to relate, were not a
History, but a piece of Poetry, and would sound to common
ears like a Fable." The remark puzzled Dr. Johnson.
"Browne," he writes, "traversed no unknown seas, or
Arabian deserts; and surely a man may visit France and

Italy, reside at Montpellier and Padua, and at last take his degree at Leyden, without any thing miraculous." But the miracles of Browne's life were miracles of the spirit. "We carry with us the wonders we seek without us." In religion he was a member of the Church of England and a very tolerant member. Singularly untroubled by religious doubt, he lived happily within the framework of this Church, and accepted its doctrines without conflict of mind. "Methinks there be not impossibilities enough in Religion for an active faith. . . . I love to lose myself in a mystery, to pursue my Reason to an *O Altitudo.*" He could surrender without a pang a belief condemned by his Church as heretical, not because he was indifferent, but because he was skeptical of the power of human reason in supernatural inquiry. He would have held with Sir John Harington that a man does better to believe a great deal more than he need rather than anything less than he ought, the one being "surely pardonable" but the other "doubtless very damnable."

Utterly naïve and innocent in theology, exposed to all the winds that blow from Greek, Christian, Jewish, and Hermetic quarters, he was attacked for the laxity of his opinions by Alexander Ross, vicar of Carisbrooke, in his *Medicus Medicatus: Or The Physician's Religion cured, by a Lenitive or Gentle Potion* (1645). Browne's charity to papists and his observation that he has no genius to dispute in religion prompt Ross's rejoinder that not to dispute against a heretic is not to fight against an enemy. And to Browne's remark that he followed the great wheel of the Church by which he moves, the captious Ross replied that the wheel was sometimes out of order, and that if Browne had been a member of the Hebrew Church when it worshiped the Calf, he would have moved with her, and danced to her pipe. Once more, when Browne says that the fatal necessity of the Stoics is nothing else but the immutable law of God's will, Ross answers:

> Is this your Religion, to make God the authour of sin, and to take away from man totally the liberty of his will? But this you doe, if you make the *Stoicall* necessity the same that the immutable law of Gods will is; for the *Stoicks* held, that what man did, whether it was good or evill, hee did it by an *inevitable necessity*, to which not onely men, but even *Jupiter* himselfe was subject. . . . This is the Religion of the *Turkes* at this day, if you will beleeve *Busbequius*: but I did not think it had been the Religion of a Christian Physician till now.

Clearly we must not look for logic and sound theology in the *Religio*. The author is modest and ingenuous enough to disclaim any opinions that do not square with maturer judgments.

An ardent and unquestioning fideist in religion, he is in philosophy curious and skeptical. He does not indeed lose his sense of wonder, and unlike Bacon he does not keep his religion and his science apart. "There is in these works of nature . . . something Divine, and hath more in it than the eye of a common spectator doth discover." He will gladly accept any dogma that his Church offers him, but in that wide and spacious country where conjecture was permissible, no man more curious in speculation, no man more eager in hazarding a conjecture. As a man of science he demands complete freedom to pursue his inquiries where they may lead him, but that there could be incompatibility between science and religion is inconceivable to him. And so in searching the secrets of nature he seems to combine relentless curiosity with an ecstatic wonder.

Browne shared with so many men of his age the belief that the world was approaching its end. But he does not believe, as Raleigh and others believed, that because the world had grown old it was in decay. There is an optimism in this book which is not found in Raleigh or in Donne, and this appears nowhere more clearly than in his remarks upon death. It has no terrors for him. In one place he tells us, "There are few that fear the face of death less than myself," and in another he says that it is not death he fears so much as the disfigurement of death, and adds with cheerful irony, "Not that I am ashamed of the Anatomy of my parts . . . whereby I might not call myself as wholesome a morsel for the worms as any." It is worlds removed from the tormented reflections of Donne upon mortality. So confident is Browne of salvation, he tells us, that he has fixed his contemplations on Heaven and almost forgotten the Idea of Hell. And so his imagination lingers not upon the gruesome trappings of death but upon the strange processes of nature, the mysteries of an incorporeal soul in a corporeal body, and the life beyond death.

He cannot be called a mystic, but the world he lived in and practiced his experiments upon seemed to him a divine world, the visible world a picture of the invisible. He collects his divinity not from the word of God but from His works. Between the visible and the invisible worlds there was continual traffic, traffic of devils as well as of angels, so much so that those who disbelieve in witches, he held, "not only deny them but Spirits; and are obliquely and upon consequence a sort not of Infidels but Atheists."

In the great Chain of Being he is a profound believer, and in man as

> that amphibious piece between a corporal and spiritual Essence, that middle form that links those two together, and makes good the Method of God and Nature, that jumps not from extreams, but unites the incompatible distances by some middle and participating natures. That we are the breath and similitude of God, it is indisputable, and upon record of Holy Scripture; but to call ourselves a Microcosm, or little World, I thought it onely a pleasant trope of Rhetorick, till my neer judgment and second thoughts told me there was a real truth therein. For first we are a rude mass, and in the rank of creatures, which onely are, and have a dull kind of being, not yet priviledged with life, or preferred to sense or reason; next we live the life of Plants, the life of Animals, the life of Men, and at last the life of Spirits, running on in one mysterious nature those five kinds of existences, which comprehend the creatures, not onely of the World, but of the Universe. Thus is Man that great and true *Amphibium,* whose nature is disposed to live, not onely like other creatures in divers elements, but in divided and distinguished worlds: for though there be but one to sense, there are two to reason, the one visible, the other invisible.

And so Nature to Browne was not inanimate. She was the Art of God, and the study of that Art was the ruling passion of his life. He realized that he was living in an age when man was discovering more and more about this Art, an age of the exantlation of Truth, the drawing up of Truth as out of a well. It was a cold thought to him that he could not hope to live to see more of this exantlation.

The *Religio Medici* brought its author fame, a European fame. Before his death it was translated into Latin, French, and "High and Low Dutch," and was known throughout Europe. But his most erudite work, and his longest, his chief contribution to science, is the folio volume entitled *Pseudodoxia Epidemica, Or, Enquiries into very many received Tenents and commonly presumed Truths,* usually referred to by its shorter title, the *Vulgar Errors.* He is here undertaking a task recommended by Bacon in the *Advancement of Learning,* an examination of fables and popular errors and the calling of them down. Others had called them down before Browne. For example, John Melton in his *Astrologaster* of 1620 had given "A Catalogue of Many Superstitious Ceremonies." Some of these have perhaps died out. In some, few of us will have difficulty in believing, as that "it is a very ill sign to be Melancholy" or that "it is a great sign of ill luck, if Rats gnaw a man's clothes." Many retain their potency in the twentieth century. Who shall say how many men and women today feel some concern if a hare crosses their path or one magpie, if they meet a black cat early in the day, if they stumble as they come out-of-doors in a morning, if the crickets desert the chimney corner, if the salt-cellar falls toward them, if they receive from their sweethearts a present of a pair of knives? To the contrary, how many are delighted if walking in the fields they find "any four-leaved grass" or if a child (like David Copperfield) be born with a caul on his head? And how many still interpret the burning of their cheek or ear as a sign that somebody somewhere is talking of them? And is it not regarded as an infallible sign of rain if a cat washes her face over her ear? If many can believe in them today, it is not surprising that they held sway three centuries ago when medicine and science were so largely empirical, and when nature was believed to have many occult qualities, sympathies, and antipathies.

George Hakewill is another writer who attacks vulgar errors before Browne. I have already referred to his book *An Apology or Declaration of the Power and Providence of God* as the first full-scale attack in English on the doctrine of the decay of Nature and the approaching dissolution of the world. In assessing the achievements of the ancients and the moderns it is very much to his purpose to expose the errors of antiquity in divinity, philosophy, and history, as well natural history as ecclesiastical and civil. And in exposing vulgar errors in natural history he covers some of the ground covered by Browne twenty years later. Beliefs that have inspired many a poet to immortal verse are now threatened:

> this pale faint swan
> Who chants a doleful hymn to his own death,
> And from the organ-pipe of frailty sings
> His soul and body to their lasting rest;

or "the kind life-rendering pelican," that repasts her young with her blood; or the very existence of the phoenix,

> . . . the bird of loudest lay
> On the sole Arabian tree.

These and other vulgar errors—as that bears lick their young into shape, that the lion trembles at the crowing of the cock, that the mole has no eyes and the elephant no knees—are in Hakewill and in Browne, but whereas Hakewill gives no more than a chapter (I.1.5) to what is to him only an incidental example of man's tenacity in retaining doctrines contrary to truth and reason, Browne gives to the theme a folio.

His first book on the causes of human error may owe something to Bacon's analysis of the varieties and causes of human error; but Browne takes his own way and makes his own divisions: for example, misapprehension, fallacy, false deduction, credulity, supinity (inertness of mind), the endeavors of Satan. Some of the most interesting, and to some readers of Browne the most surprising, chapters in this first book are the attacks on adherence to antiquity, tradition, and authority. In any battle between the ancients and the moderns Browne sides with the moderns. He does not find much to admire in the apophthegms of the ancients; and their adages, he maintains, may be paralleled if not exceeded by those of more unlearned nations and many of our own. And he utterly condemns the practice of introducing the testimony of ancient writers to confirm commonplaces which no reasonable hearer would dissent from. Moreover, he points out with some relish some of the errors of the ancients which had been exposed by the advancement of knowledge in recent years.

In this book Browne is then in one sense a modern man of science, undertaking a task recommended by Bacon, a task which the Royal Society in its early years did not consider to be beneath its dignity. Indeed, to some conservative minds Browne was much too ready to dismiss beliefs hallowed by the authority of the ancients. Alexander Ross, an ardent Aristotelian and supporter of lost causes, who attacked Browne for heresy in the *Religio Medici*, attacked him again as a modern innovator misconstruing the "dictates and opinions of the ancient champions of learning." (*Arcana Microcosmi: Or, The hid Secrets of Man's Body disclosed,* 1651.) Ross makes no question that there are or have been griffins and centaurs, and unicorns in whose horns are occult qualities against poison. He believes that Browne would not doubt that some men become speechless at sight of a wolf if he had himself ever been surprised by one. Some lions, if not all, are certainly afraid of a cock; and why not, when the elephant is frightened by a hog, and the monkey trembles at sight of a gammon of bacon? It is folly to deny that the female viper bites off the head of the sire in the act of generation and that in revenge the young vipers eat their way out of their mother's vitals. And to question whether mice can be procreated of putrefaction is to question Reason, Sense, and Experience. And so the wrongheaded Ross proceeds to his conclusion with a metaphor drawn from a vulgar error:

> I pity to see so many young heads, still gaping like Chamelions for knowledge, and are never filled, because they feed upon airy and empty phansies, loathing the sound, solid, and wholsome viands of Peripatetick wisdome, they reject Aristotles pure Fountains, and dig to themselves cisterns that will hold no water.

But the attempt to set up Browne as a modern man of science, even in that age when the medieval and the modern were still inextricably mingled, is beyond my power. His aims and many of his conclusions are modern, yet in method and in style nothing could be more remote from the course that science was taking when Browne wrote his book. In spite of what he says in the first book, he delights to parade the authority of the ancients, classical and medieval. The *Vulgar Errors,* it has been said, "is the twilight of the medieval gods." Albertus Magnus and other "learned and authentic fellows" make almost their last appearances as serious authorities on matters of science. He cites them even if he contradicts them, so lingering at his task of demolition and killing his errors as if he loved them. Contrast Hakewill's swift despatch of the belief that when bees lose their stings they turn into drones: "*Virgil* tells us, that together with their stings they lose their life. *Animamque in vulnere ponunt.* And Mr. Butler a great Beemaster in his *Feminine Monarchy* hath observed, that the drones are such by kind, not by accident." Centuries of error disappear at a touch.

Many of the errors Browne examines are not susceptible to experiment, but they invite speculation. He delights in hazarding a wide solution, admitting a wavering conjecture. On one occasion he wrote to Sir William Dugdale: "in points of . . . obscurity probable possibilities must suffice for truth," and he is happiest in that realm where conjecture can never be overtaken by proof, happiest when wandering "in the America and untravelled parts of truth."

In a way he prefers observation and experiment to authority. He dismisses the view that moles have no eyes by saying—as Hakewill had argued before him—"that they have eyes in their head is manifest unto any, that wants them not in his own." Yet he does not always resort to observation and experiment when these were desirable and possible. The stock example and the best is his treatment of the problem whether badgers have the legs on one side shorter than on the other (3.5). First, the authority of Albertus Magnus and Aldrovandus is against it.

> Again, It seems no easie affront unto Reason, and generally repugnant unto the course of Nature: for if we survey the total set of Animals, we may in their legs, or Organs of progression, observe an equality of length, and a parity of Numeration; that is, not any to have an odd legg, or the supporters and movers of one side not exactly answered by the other. Although the hinder may be unequal unto the fore and middle legs, as in Frogs, Locusts, and Grashoppers; or both unto the middle, as in some Beetles and Spiders, as is determined by Aristotle, *De incessu Animalium*. Perfect and viviparous quadrupeds, so standing in their position of proneness, that the opposite joints of Neighbour-legs consist in the same plane; and a line descending from their Navel intersects at right angles the axis of the Earth. It happeneth often I confess that a Lobster hath the Chely or great claw of one side longer than the other; but this is not properly their leg, but a part of apprehension, and whereby they hold or seize upon their prey; for the legs and proper parts of progression are inverted backward, and stand in a position opposite unto these.
>
> Lastly, The Monstrosity is ill contrived, and with some disadvantage; the shortness being affixed unto the legs of one side, which might have been more

tolerably placed upon the thwart or Diagonal Movers. For the progression of quadrupeds being performed *per Diametrum*, that is the cross legs moving or resting together, so that two are always in motion, and two in station at the same time; the brevity had been more tolerable in the cross legs; For then the Motion and station had been performed by equal legs; whereas herein they are both performed by unequal Organs, and the imperfection becomes discoverable at every hand.

No prose can be more different from that exacted from its members by the Royal Society. Where Browne supposes that within a few years it will be necessary to learn Latin in order to understand English, they demand "a close, naked, natural way of speaking" and prefer the language of artisans, countrymen, and merchants to that of wits or scholars. Was Browne never a member of the Royal Society because his style disqualified him? I used to think so, but now I am not so sure. In those days it was not difficult to secure election. Some of the poets were members—Denham, Waller, Dryden—and many a gentleman who had not a tithe of Browne's learning. And if we look at the early Transactions of the Society we find ourselves at times in a world rather congenial to the author of *Vulgar Errors*. For example, "The Duke of Buckingham promised to bring into the Society a piece of a unicorn's horn." He did so, and they made a circle of the powder of the horn, and used it to test the popular belief that if the horn were genuine a spider would be charmed to remain within the circle, such was the antipathy between the spider and the unicorn. The record of the experiment was that the spider "immediately ran out several times repeated. The spider once made some stay upon the powder."

Now Browne would have been an ornament to the society. He was a very considerable antiquary, and a learned botanist, zoölogist, and ornithologist, and of course accomplished in medical science. John Evelyn, F.R.S., made a special journey to Norwich, he tells us, "having a desire to see that famous scholar and physician Dr. T. Browne . . . with whom I had sometime corresponded by letters, though never saw before, whose whole house and garden being a paradise and cabinet of rarities, and that of the best collection, especially medals, books, plants, natural things, did exceedingly refresh me." Another fellow, John Ray, acknowledged the help which he received in compiling a catalogue of English birds "from the learned and deservedly famous Sir Thomas Browne of Norwich."

Why then did he not join the society? Here is my guess. First, he had less worldly ambition than most men. Pope writes satirically of those who "shine in the dignity of F.R.S.," but it was no temptation to Browne to join a society for the sake of a label. Moreover, when the society received its royal charter in 1662, Browne's fame was already established. Secondly, he hardly left Norwich from the time he settled there. So he could not have attended the meetings. And lastly, he knew what the society was doing without joining it. Certainly he did not refrain for the reason that Roger North's brother, Lord Keeper Guilford, refrained —because the wits of the town were making free with the society and because "he could not discover what advantage of knowledge could come to him that way which he could not arrive at otherwise." Browne corresponded with the secretary and with fellows of the society, and his son Edward became a fellow when a young London physician, and was encouraged by his father to be of service to the society. And so like a wise man he stayed at home, cultivated his garden and made of it a paradise, saved his dues, and joined no societies at all.

Many of Browne's letters have survived. Among his correspondents were Sir William Dugdale, John Evelyn, Christopher Merrett the naturalist, John Aubrey. And there are many letters of fatherly advice to his sons, the sailor and the physician. Here is the same interest in out-of-the-way learning and in problems that can never be experimented upon: "What kind of stone is that which stoned St. Stephen, pebble, flint, or freestone?" Here is the same relish for conjecture; when Dugdale inquires about a fish, Browne asks him to send it: "I shall not be backward in my conjecture." Here is the same interest in vulgar errors. In his book he tells us that though he had seen an ostrich he had not had the opportunity of testing by experiment the belief that the ostrich could digest iron. Many years later his son acquired an ostrich, and gave him the opportunity. He writes: "If you give any Iron, it may be wrapped up in dough or paste: perhaps it will not take it up alone." But the bird died, and they brought in a verdict against the climate of London. In these letters we see Browne the scholar or Browne the father, but not Browne the master of English prose. Of the subtle and elaborate music of his deliberately written works there is hardly a trace. For example, any father might have written this to any son: "You are mightily improved in your violin; but I would by no means have you practice upon the trumpet for many reasons."

For his greatest prose we turn to *Hydriotaphia, Urn Burial,* and *The Garden of Cyrus,* published together and in that order in a small octavo volume in 1658. The one is about the various methods of burial in ancient times, the other about quincunxes in Heaven and on earth, in nature and in the mind of man. Professor F. L. Huntley has shown that their conjunction is not fortuitous. "One concerns death, the other life; one the body, the other the soul; one passions, the other reason; one accident, the other design; one substance, the other form." And in Browne's own words, "That we conjoin these parts of different subjects . . . your judgment will admit without impute of incongruity; since the delightful world comes after death, and Paradise succeeds the Grave." Browne was a learned man, but modern scholars have discovered that in writing these books he used books of reference, short cuts to learning, without always troubling to indicate the source or nature of his borrowings. The practice is not unknown today. But we do not go to these works for their learning. He was inspired to write *Urn Burial* by the discovery of some urns at Walsingham which he took to be Roman. They were Saxon, yet the value of his book is no more invalidated by advances in archaeology than is the value of the *Compleat Angler* by advances, if there have been any, in piscatorial science. His learning could be borrowed, but not his vision. When Ross mentioned the "obliquities" of the *Religio Medici,* he had in mind Browne's innocent heresies. When Charles Lamb praised

Browne's "beautiful obliquities," he had in mind the un-expectedness of his thought. His mind is like a seventeenth-century perspective glass which made what was awry look straight and what was straight look awry.

The danger with a man like Browne, no very clear or profound thinker yet with a style so elaborate, is when the matter is not answerable to the style, when the reader becomes aware of a discrepancy between the poverty of the thought and the pomp of language and cadence expended on it. In *Urn Burial* his themes are all common-places: the decay and dissolution of all material things, the vanities of man, the transience of the monuments of human power, time and immortality, life and death. But they stir and provoke his mind as he turns them over and over, looks upon them now from one surprising angle and now from another, and makes what was old seem new by the obliquity of his vision and the strange majesty of his style. Take him, for example, upon the approaching dissolution of the world, a belief which he shared with many writers, though opposition to his view from the realms of religion and of science was increasing. The world in his belief would last but 6,000 years from the time of its creation, and of these some 5,600 had elapsed. The future, then, was small compared with the past, and time had long since passed its meridian.

> And therefore restless inquietude for the diuturnity of our memories unto present considerations, seemes a vanity almost out of date, and superannuated peece of folly. We cannot hope to live so long in our names, as some have done in their persons, one face of Janus

holds no proportion to the other. 'Tis too late to be ambitious. The great mutations of the world are acted, or time may be too short for our designes. To extend our memories by Monuments, whose death we dayly pray for, and whose duration we cannot hope, without injury to our expectations, in the advent of the last day, were a contradiction to our beliefs. We whose generations are ordained in this setting part of time, are providentially taken off from such imaginations. And being necessitated to eye the remaining particle of futurity, are naturally constituted unto thoughts of the next world, and cannot excusably decline the consideration of that duration, which maketh Pyramids pillars of snow, and all that's past a moment. . . .

Oblivion is not to be hired: The greater part must be content to be as though they had not been, to be found in the register of God, not in the record of man. Twenty seven names make up the first story [before the Flood], and the recorded names ever since contain not one living Century. The number of the dead long exceedeth all that shall live. The night of time far surpasseth the day, and who knows when was the Æquinox? Every houre addes unto that current Arithmetique, which scarce stands one moment. And since death must be the Lucina of life, and even Pagans could doubt whether thus to live, were to die; Since our longest Sun sets at right descensions, and makes but winter arches, and therefore it cannot be long before we lie down in darknesse, and have our light in ashes; Since the brother of death daily haunts us with dying *memento's,* and time that grows old it self, bids us hope no long duration: Diuturnity is a dream and folly of expectation.

It is a slow, solemn progress. Unlike so many of his contemporaries, and particularly unlike Robert Burton, he does not interlace his prose with quotations. One reason may be that he decried the citation of ancient sayings which do not exceed "the extemporall sententiosity" of our own common conceit; but the chief reason may be that he wished to keep the current of his own prose clear and uninterrupted. In the whole of *Urn Burial* I find but two quotations. One of them, from Lucan, ends the book, so that in a sense it lies outside his own prose. The other, from Tibullus, comes at the end of the famous first paragraph of the famous fifth chapter: *Sic ego componi versus in ossa velim,* "Thus I when turned into bones would wish to be laid to rest." I cannot do better than end by quoting this paragraph. One gloss is necessary. Because he believed that the urns were Roman, he speaks of the drums and tramplings of *three* conquests: the Saxons, the Danes, the Normans.

Now since these dead bones have already out-lasted the living ones of Methuselah, and in a yard under ground, and thin walls of clay, out-worn all the strong and specious buildings above it; and quietly rested under the drums and tramplings of three conquests; What Prince can promise such diuturnity unto his Reliques, or might not gladly say,

Sic ego componi versus in ossa velim.

V

The Sermon

For the greater part of the seventeenth century everyone went to church; everyone had to go to church or pay the fines for recusancy. The consequence to the preacher was that he was always sure of a congregation, and often a crowded congregation; the consequence to the congregation was not only that they were instructed in Christian doctrine but that they became, some of them, highly conscious critics of the preacher's rhetoric. Those who had been educated at grammar school and university had of course been trained in the art of rhetoric and so would be better-informed judges than are most of us today of the preacher's invention or choice of subject matter, of the disposition or logical arrangement of the subject matter, of his elocution or use of tropes and figures, and of his pronunciation, the management of voice and gesture. We may remind ourselves that some of those who attended church also attended the theater where they were as conscious critics of invention, disposition, elocution, and pronunciation, as they were in church.

The point may be illustrated by reference to two diarists, John Manningham and John Evelyn, who between them cover the greater part of the century. Manningham was admitted to the Middle Temple in 1597 and was granted the degree of an utter barrister in 1605. His diary covers the years 1602–1603 and is chiefly remembered for its reference to a performance of *Twelfth Night* at his inn in 1602. Cheek by jowl with jests of such a nature that his nineteenth-century editor felt obliged to omit them, he set down the heads of sermons he attended with notes on the preachers. He was interested, as a budding barrister would be, in invention and disposition, and sometimes he criticized the preacher's delivery and appearance. One preacher he condemned as inaudible. Another, whose sermon was a strong continued invective against the papists, was observed to have a long brown beard, a hanging look, a gloating eye, and a tossing, leering gesture. At Paul's Cross, the cathedral's famous open-air pulpit, a preacher wore a velvet nightcap which he was observed to remove when he mentioned the queen but not when he mentioned the Almighty. In the same pulpit a young man made a finical boisterous exordium and ran himself almost dry before he was half through. (Evidently he was of the same breed as Earle's "young raw preacher"—"a bird not yet fledged, that hath hopped out of his nest to be chirping on a hedge, and will be straggling abroad at what peril soever.") Manningham is surprisingly severe on Dr. John Rainolds, still remembered as Richard Hooker's tutor at Oxford, as a bitter enemy of academic or any other drama, and as one of the translators of the Authorized Version; but Manningham is probably passing judgment on him as a writer, not as a preacher. Rainolds impressed others as a man whose memory and reading were near to a miracle.

As we should expect, Evelyn is more serious and less vivid. He is also more voluminous, how voluminous we did not realize until the full text of the diary was published by E. S. de Beer in 1955. Evelyn's notes on sermons extend from about the year 1652, the year of his return from the Continent, till within a few weeks of his death in 1706, a survey of more than fifty years; and, if I may pilfer from the editor's excellent index, here are references to sermons allegorical, cabalistic, catechistical, Eucharistical, florid, historical, logical, metaphysical, passionate, penitential, philosophicotheological, poetical, rabbinical, scholastical.

The appetite of the century for sermons, the patience and the endurance with which it listened to the spoken word, puts our laggard age to shame. Sermons lasted usually for one hour, but some preachers neglected to notice if the sands in the hourglass were almost run. Isaac Barrow, we are told, was generally too long in his sermons. When he gave the Spital sermon before the mayor and aldermen he preached for three hours and a half. His theme was the "Duty and Reward of Bounty to the Poor." As printed, the sermon occupies thirty-nine folio pages. There he was in complete control, but at Westminster Abbey in holiday time when he went on preaching over his hour the congregation, anxious to see the tombs and the effigies of the kings and queens in wax, and the abbey servants anxious for their fees, caused the organ to be struck up and to continue playing "till they had blowed him down." More sympathetic was the audience of Laurence Chaderton, first master of Emmanuel College, Cambridge. Having once preached for two hours he said that he had tried his hearers' patience and would leave off, upon which the whole congregation cried out "For God's sake, sir, go on! we beg you, go on!" So he continued the thread of his discourse for another hour, "to the great pleasure and delight of his hearers." At one place sermons *had* to be short. George Meriton, parson of Hadleigh in Suffolk, published a sermon in 1607 with the warning: *"It is a short Sermon.* For it was preached, not at the *Cross,* but at the *Court:* The one place requiring length, the other expecting brevity." Why brevity was advisable at court needs no explanation. When George Montaigne, Bishop of London, preached on Christmas Day, 1622, James I took exception and "grew loud," so that the bishop was driven to end abruptly, perhaps because he had spoken too much. Burnet tells us that Charles II liked his sermons clear, plain, and short. Why length was tolerated at Paul's Cross may be because it was easier than in the cathedral itself to slink away without notice. In his *Memorial of William Lamb* (*ca.* 1580) Abraham Fleming gave Lamb this praise:

> he hath bene seene and marked at Powles crosse, to haue continued from eight of the clocke, vntill eleuen, attentiuely listening to the Preachers voice, and to haue endured the ende, being weake and aged, when others both strong and lustie went away.

By 1640 the Bishop of London was giving instructions that a preacher at the Cross was not to exceed an hour and a half in both sermon and prayer.

Sermons were read as well as listened to. It has been calculated that of the books known to have been published

in England before 1641 nearly half are books of moral
philosophy and religion. It has also been reckoned that in
Elizabeth's reign alone at least 1,200 sermons were published, not counting reprints. The demand for printed sermons by popular preachers was so great that some were
taken down by shorthand and published in garbled versions.
The sermons of Henry Smith received this honor. He died
in 1591, but the appeal of his popular rhetoric was so great
that his sermons were still being reprinted nearly a hundred
years later. "Silver-tongued" is the epithet attached to him
by contemporaries: as Fuller said, only one metal lower
than St. Chrysostom.

A passage in Burton's *Anatomy* gives us a good idea of
the plethora of printed sermons. He is explaining why he,
a divine, has chosen to write about melancholy. He acknowledges that divinity is the queen of professions, but, he says,

> in Divinitie I saw no such great need. For had I written
> positively, there be so many books in that kinde, so
> many commentators, treatises, pamphlets, expositions,
> sermons, that whole teemes of oxen cannot draw them;
> and had I been as forward and ambitious as some
> others, I might have haply printed a sermon at *Pauls-
> Crosse,* a sermon in St. *Maries Oxon.,* a sermon in
> *Christ-Church,* or a sermon before the right honour-
> able, right reverend, a sermon before the right wor-
> shipfull, a sermon in latine, in english, a sermon with a
> name, a sermon without, a sermon, a sermon, &c.

As bewildering as the number of sermons is their variety.
There are sermons plain and colored, Attic and Asiatic,
simple and learned, dry and watery, dialectical and rhetorical. Is it possible to prophesy from a man's creed what style
of sermon he would preach? Not very surely. If he were a

Calvinist within the Church of England, he might prefer a style that is bare, or almost bare, of tropes and figures. So William Perkins, who though he died in 1602 cannot be neglected in any account of the seventeenth-century sermon, for his influence on the "saints" of England and New England was deep and durable. He held that for the proving of his high argument logic was a better tool than rhetoric. He expounded the doctrines of predestination, imputed righteousness, or external damnation with as much bareness as the difficulty of his themes permitted, displaying, says Joseph Hall, "a distinct judgment and a rare dexterity in clearing the obscure subtleties of the school, and easy explication of the most perplex discourses." His method was strictly scholastic. He permitted no learned adornments to interrupt the progress of his thought. Sometimes he supports an argument by reference to the Fathers or (rarely) to some modern instance of sin and punishment, but to find in his text or margin any tincture of pagan learning or pagan philosophy is most unusual. He believed learning necessary to a preacher, but not the display of it. So in his *Art of Prophesying*, a manual for many a New England pastor:

> *Humane wisdome* must be concealed, whether it be in the matter of the sermon, or in the setting forth of the words; because the preaching of the word is the *Testimonie of God, and the profession of the knowledge of Christ,* and not of humane skill: and againe, because the hearers ought not to ascribe their faith to the gifts of men, but to the power of Gods word.

It is in the main true that the dialectical was most favored by preachers of the stricter sort. (In this lecture I am trying to avoid the use of the word "puritan," which means several

different things at one time and several different other
things at another time.) The schoolmen used to compare
logic to the fist, and rhetoric to the palm of the hand, logic
having a close pressing form of proceeding, rhetoric a
dilated and loose open way of expression. The clenched
fist of syllogistical argument was used by a preacher at
Paul's Cross in 1577 when he attacked the theater in these
terms: "the cause of plagues is sin, if you look to it well:
and the cause of sin are plays: therefore the cause of
plagues are plays." More elaborate examples of what Marvell calls "syllogistical legerdemain" may be found in the
works of William Prynne who preached not from the pulpit
but from the press. In 1628, when there was a fashion among
men for wearing the hair long, and among women for wearing the hair short, he wrote an acrimonious pamphlet the
title of which is too long to quote in full:

> The Vnlouelinesse, of Love-Lockes. *Or,* A summarie
> Discourse proouing: *The wearing, and nourishing of
> a Locke, or Loue-Locke, to be altogether vnseemely,
> and vnlawfull vnto Christians.* In which there are like-
> wise some passages . . . against Face-painting; the
> wearing of Supposititious, Poudred, Frizled, or extraor-
> dinary long Haire; the inordinate affectation of cor-
> porall Beautie; and Womens Mannish, Vnnaturall,
> Impudent, and vnchristian cutting of their Haire; the
> Epidemicall Vanities, and Vices of our Age.

He proves his case by a series of syllogisms.

> [The major premise:] That which is an ordinary,
> and common Badge, or Embleme of Effeminacy, Pride,
> Vaine-Glory, Lasciuiousnesse, Inciuilitie, Licentious-

nesse, and Deboistnesse: must needes be Odious, Vnseemely, and Vnlawfull vnto Christians.

[The minor premise:] But the wearing, and nourish-
ing of these Loue-lockes, is an ordinary, and common
Badge, or Embleme of Effeminacy, Pride, Vaine-glory,
Lasciuiousnesse, Inciuilitie, Licentiousnesse, and Deboistnesse.

[The conclusion:] *Therefore it must needes be
Odious, Vnseemely, and Vnlawfull vnto Christians.*

The Maior is irrefragable, . . . The Minor, shall
backe and fortifie: . . . must bee granted, and the
conclusion too.

But not all Calvinists were content to give logic the
preëminence over rhetoric. The Jacobean Thomas Adams
succeeded the Elizabethan Henry Smith as a popular London preacher. Like Perkins he was a Calvinist in Anglican
orders but his sermons are much colored by simile and metaphor, proverb and homely example and illustration. He
keeps up to date and on terms with his congregation by introducing into his sermons elaborate Theophrastan characters, and he is fond of quoting the classics. Perhaps
preachers may be divided into three classes according as
they freely admitted quotations from and allusions to the
classics, forbade the use of all human wisdom (like Perkins), or admitted occasional reference to heathen sayings
for the purpose of convincing atheists or shaming those
who professed themselves Christians. There was much controversy on these points. In the *Directory for the Public
Worship of God* of 1644 the preacher was ordered to ab-
stain "from an unprofitable use of unknown tongues, strange
phrases, and cadences of sounds and words, sparingly citing

sentences of ecclesiastical or other human writers, ancient or modern, be they never so elegant."

We may find it surprising that the popular preacher and Calvinist Thomas Adams should often quote the classics, whereas the learned High-Church preachers Andrewes and Donne should seldom do so. More unexpected still is the fact that learned sermons had a dangerous attraction for the illiterate. The Restoration divine, Robert South, said that those who were fondest of high-flown metaphors and allegories, attended and set off with scraps of Greek and Latin, were ignorant and illiterate country people. It is on record that the parishioners of the notable orientalist Edward Pococke, whose life almost spans the century (1604–1691) and whose learning was the admiration of Europe, actually complained that he did not in his sermons quote Greek and Latin and Hebrew. "Our Parson," they said to an Oxford friend of his, "is a plain honest man; but Master, he is no Latiner." The same principle lies behind the story of the old woman who told her pastor that she found great solace in that comfortable word Mesopotamia. Of rather different application is the story of Dr. John Aylmer, Bishop of London, who is said to have had a notable art of winning the ears of his auditors. Once when he perceived them not so attentive as they should have been, he fell to reading the Hebrew bible. Now thoroughly awake they gazed at him with amazement, and after a grave reprimand he went on with his sermon.

So far I have been trying to indicate the wealth of sermon literature in the century, and the variety, by dipping a little pail into this vast ocean and bringing up a few specimens.

I turn now to consider a few of the preachers whose sermons
are still read and valued by some. A book on the *Art and
Method of Preaching* by William Chappell (1656) has at
the end a bibliography of sermons, and one heading in this
bibliography is "Elaborate Sermons." Among the names that
appear under this heading are those of Lancelot Andrewes,
John Donne, and Jeremy Taylor. Andrewes and Donne are
the most distinguished preachers of the High-Church movement. Many of Andrewes' sermons were preached before
critical audiences at court, many of Donne's at court or in
his cathedral of St. Paul's. Both were influenced by much
the same models in sermon rhetoric, held much the same
doctrine, addressed often enough the same audience, yet
no one could mistake a sermon by Andrewes for one by
Donne.

For every reader of Andrewes there are, I suppose, a
hundred of Donne. The University of California Press is
publishing an admirable edition of Donne's sermons, but I
have not heard of proposals for an edition of Andrewes.
One reason why the one is so much more read than the
other may be that John Donne was once Jack Donne,
whereas Andrewes was always Lancelot. Another is that
many who are fascinated by Donne's poetry turn to the
sermons in search of the same subtle wit, the same play
of logic and passion, maybe the same macabre treatment
of the trappings of death and the odor of dissolution. And
a third reason is that Donne is the darling of anthologists.
If we read him in Pearsall Smith's selections and there only,
we must suppose that he never teased his text, never
brought to bear the full weight of patristic and scholastic

learning, never preached the sober prose of plain exposition. Nevertheless, what Donne does, and Andrewes never, is to kindle into eloquence, the eloquence of a man with a subtle feeling for the texture of words and for periodic structure, the clauses as they ascend to their climax opening out and closing in to capture the ear with the beauty of their varied rhythms.

> If some King of the earth have so large an extent of Dominion, in North, and South, as that he hath Winter and Summer together in his Dominions, so large an extent East and West, as that he hath day and night together in his Dominions, much more hath God mercy and judgement together: He brought light out of darknesse, not out of a lesser light; he can bring thy Summer out of Winter, though thou have no Spring; though in the wayes of fortune, or understanding, or conscience, thou have been benighted till now, wintred and frozen, clouded and eclypsed, damped and benummed, smothered and stupified till now, now God comes to thee, not as in the dawning of the day, nor as in the bud of the spring, but as the Sun at noon to illustrate all shadowes, as the sheaves in harvest, to fill all penuries, all occasions invite his mercies, and all times are his seasons.

The passage was praised by that great taster of literature and wine, George Saintsbury, as perhaps unequaled. It is a mark of the delicacy and subtlety of the rhythm that the ear is jarred if we give to the word "illus'trate" its modern pronunciation.

What of the danger that a man may become more interested in the preacher himself than in his message? Donne was aware of it. The Devil, he says, comes to church, "some-

times to work an affectation in the speaker, and many times
doth more harm by a good Sermon then by a weak, by pos-
sessing the hearers with an admiration of the Preacher's
gifts, and neglecting God's ordinance." With Andrewes
there is no temptation to be more interested in the preacher
than the doctrine. He provides one of the worst models of
pulpit oratory a modern preacher could set himself to imitate. Indeed no preacher in possession of his wits would
choose to follow Andrewes, although he might model himself on Tillotson or Barrow or South and still remain at
large. Yet Andrewes is one of the greatest preachers that
ever graced an Anglican pulpit, and the loss in power and
passion as we compare his sermons with Tillotson's is very
great. I choose as an example a passage from the sermon
preached at court on Christmas Day, 1622, a sermon which
has inspired T. S. Eliot's poem "The Journey of the Magi."
It has to be a passage of some length, for only so can justice
be done to the steady march of logic and passion. Andrewes
repeatedly refers to two words in his text: "there came
Wise Men," *venimus;* and "we have seen his star," *vidimus
stellam.*

It is not commended, to stand *gazing vp into heauen*
too long, on Christ Himselfe ascending: much lesse
on His star. For, they sate not still gazing on the star.
Their *Vidimus* begat *Venimus;* their seeing made them
come; come a long journey. *Venimus* is soone sayd;
but a *short word:* But, many a wide and weary step
they made, before they could come to say *Venimus,*
Lo, *here we are come; Come* and at our journeys end.
To look a little on it. In this their *Comming,* we
consider, First, the distance of the Place, they came

from. It was not hard by, as the *shepherds* (but a
step to Bethlehem, over the fields:) This was riding
many a hundred miles, and cost them many a days
journey. Secondly, we consider the *Way*, that they
came: If it be *pleasant*, or plaine and *easy*: For, if
it be, it is so much the better. This was nothing *pleasant;* for, through *desarts*, all the way waste and deso-
late. Nor (secondly) *easy* neither: For, over the rocks
and crags of both *Arabies* (specially *Petrea*) their
journey lay. Thirdly, yet if *safe:* But it was not; but
exceeding dangerous, a lying through the middest of
the *Blacke Tents of Kedar*, a Nation of *Theeves* and
Cut-throats; to passe over the *hills* of *Robbers;* Infamous then, and infamous to this day. No passing,
without great troop, or convoy. Last we consider the
time of their *comming*, the season of the yeare. It
was no *summer progresse*. A cold *comming* they had
of it, at this time of the yeare: just the worst time of
the yeare, to take a journey, and specially a long
journey in. The waies deep, the weather sharp, the
daies short, the sun farthest off *in solstitio brumali*,
the very dead of *Winter*. *Venimus*, Wee are come,
if that be one; *Venimus*, Wee are (now) come, come
at this time, that (sure) is another.

And these difficulties they overcame, of a *weari-
some, irksome, troublesome, dangerous, unseasonable*
journey; And for all this, they *came*. And, came it
cherefully, and quickly; As appeareth, by the speed
they made. It was but *Vidimus, Venimus,* with them;
They *saw*, and they *came:* No sooner *saw*, but they
set out presently. . . .

And wee, what should we have done? Sure, these
men of the *East* shall rise in Judgement against the
men of the West, that is, us: and their faith, against
ours, in this point. With them, it was but *Vidimus,
Venimus:* With us, it would have beene but *Veniemus*
at most. Our fashion is, to see and see againe, before
we stirre a foot: Specially, if it be to the worship of
Christ. Come such a Journey, at such a time? No: but

fairely have put it off to the Spring of the yeare, till
the dayes longer, and the wayes fairer, and the weather
warmer; till better travelling to Christ. Our *Epiphanie*
would (sure) have fallen in *Easter-weeke* at the
soonest.

Looked at from one point of view the style reaches the
height of Senecan vanity, or the vanity of those church
Fathers who followed the writers of Silver Latin. There is
the paradoxical antithetical wit, the quibbling with sense
and sometimes with words, the advance by a series of short
sentences. So strong is the forward movement, the sequa-
ciousness, that he can be as elliptical as he likes, omit verbs
and connecting particles, yet never leave his meaning and
the development of it obscure. And while the language is
taut and spare, so that the reader can never relax his attention, the diction is simple and often colloquial. I have
quoted a favorable example, of course, yet many another
passage helps us to understand why his sermons at court left
behind a sting or aculeus even upon the minds of the
greatest gallants. Bacon speaks of the aculeate style, that
which stings you into attention and thought. Andrewes used
the style to goad his auditors into an active Christian life.

The attack on Andrewes' witty preaching began before he
was in his grave. Bishop Felton who died in the same year,
1626, is reported to have said: "I had almost marred my
own natural Trot by endeavouring to imitate his artificial
Amble." By the third quarter of the century a chorus of
divines is pleading for the plain style and alluding con-
temptuously to fantastic wit or the squeezing of a text. A
surprisingly late reference to a sermon in Andrewes' style

is in Evelyn's diary, July 15, 1683: "The old man preached much after Bishop Andrewes's method, full of logical divisions, in short and broken periods, and Latin sentences, now quite out of fashion in the pulpit: grown into a far more profitable way, of plain and practical." Andrewes was "practical" but far from being "plain." But before turning to the plain sermon, a word about Jeremy Taylor, the third of the "elaborate" preachers I will mention. No doubt an anthology of purple passages misrepresents him as well as Donne, if not as much as Donne. There is much plain unadorned prose in Taylor, prose of controversy and prose of casuistry. But in his own day and with critics like Lamb and Coleridge he was famous for his eloquence. One of his most fervent admirers, his anthologist Pearsall Smith, has to admit that "his mental powers were somewhat limited and commonplace." This distinguishes him sharply from Andrewes and Donne. It is again to distinguish him sharply from Andrewes and Donne to say that the characteristics of his style are suggested by words like grace, harmony, sweetness, mellifluousness; that some of the most highly wrought passages are long set pieces of description —usually in the form of simile or metaphor—images of beauty drawn more often than not from aspects of nature or human nature which recommend themselves at once as pleasurable: children, roses, the effects of light on water, and so on; that his similes, which often begin with a "Thus have I seen . . . ," are elaborated to the point where the mind abstracts itself from what is being illustrated and loses itself in the illustration. How far these images from external nature show him to have been a close observer of nature is a matter of dispute. One of the most famous of his similes is that of the silkworm, but the same simile is in the *Miscellanea* (1604) of Elizabeth Grymeston, and behind her is the visionary eye of Saint Teresa.

If I wanted to show Taylor at his best I should turn to the funeral sermon on the Countess of Carbery of Golden Grove in Carmarthenshire, especially the passage which begins, "In all her Religion, and in all her actions of relation towards God, she had a strange evenness and untroubled passage, sliding toward her Ocean of God and of infinity with a certain and silent motion. So have I seen a river. . . ." But I confess I have an imperfect sympathy with him. I find his beauties cloying and his style too jeremitaylorically purple. Even a devotee must admit that there is sometimes a discrepancy between the style and the message. In excess or in the hands of a bungler it is a disastrous style in or out of the pulpit, much more disastrous than Andrewes', because with him thought saves it from inanition.

That sermons should be "simple and perspicuous" was the belief of William Perkins and of many a preacher of the stricter sort in the age of Andrewes and of Donne. In 1603 Henry Crosse attacked the preachers who aped profane phrases, metaphors, allegories,

and so much vaine eloquence, as they yeeld no fruite at all to their auditors, but driue them into amazement with a multitude of Inkehorne-termes scummed from the Latin, . . . when the most profitable and best affected speech is that that is most congruable and fitly applied to the intendment & vnderstanding of the hearers by familiar and ordinarie termes; . . . but such as . . . be addicted to affectation, haue com-

monly a dearth of iudgement, sildome edifie, but gallop
ouer prophane writers to shewe theyr vaine reading.

In truth common sense has always demanded that sermons should be suited to the capacity of their auditors.
Popular preaching has never been defunct. A preacher ad-
dressing a simple audience in church or chapel or market
place must consider how he is to arrest a wandering attention and how best he may bring home to each member of
his congregation the message he must deliver. Whatever
the age of the sermon, whether preached by a medieval
friar or by the latest revivalist, we shall find in it a colloquial
form, homely instances, timely jests, *exempla* brought in at
the appropriate moment and usually, as with the Master
whom the preacher serves, from what lies before the audi-
tor's eyes, the occasional touch of rhetoric, especially the use
of figures that build up suspense or by repetition enforce a
moral. This was the way of John Bunyan, no doubt, who
preached without notes and did not print his sermons, but
subsumed their doctrine in his allegories and pamphlets.
And in the reign of Edward VI so preached Hugh Latimer,
a good shepherd who knew his flock individually and the
ailments that afflicted them. He knew when cobblers missed
their stitches, when clothmakers stretched their cloths to
gain an added yard of material, when judges took bribes
and gave false decisions, when servants scanted their masters' service or masters their servants' wages, when hus-
bandmen put their best corn at the top and bottom of the
sack and the worst in the middle. His eye was on the next
world, but there were few who knew this world better. He

was a popular preacher by nature, and the learned discipline of school and university could not turn him into anything else. Whether preaching at court or in parish church he had to be plain, had to be homely and colloquial. What marks him off from most popular preachers is that he was a bishop and that he is still read. His sermons may be said to rise into literature.

But who now reads the popular Puritan preachers of the seventeenth century? Who now reads John Dod, John Goodwin, John Preston, Richard Sibbes, Thomas Taylor? The answer to this rhetorical question is that Professor William Haller does. In the excellent chapter on "The Rhetoric of the Spirit" in his *Rise of Puritanism* he tells us that they did not much concern themselves with attacks on prevailing manners nor did they spend much time describing the tortures of the damned. Their main concern was to chart "in infinite detail and tireless reiteration the course of the godly soul out of hardness and indifference to the consciousness of its lost condition, and so out of despair and repentance to faith in God." And this they did in a style which only admitted imagery if it struck home by its familiarity. When they wished to praise a sermon they praised it as plain or powerful or perspicuous or pithy or all these.

These epithets are not very distinguishing. If we had put it to Bishop South that his sermons were plain, powerful, perspicuous, pithy, he would have been pleased, and we should be telling the truth. But South's sermons are evidently the work of a learned man, a man with a full mind; though he does not parade his learning, he does not conceal it, and in the sermons of the puritans all suggestion of an "esoteric or aristocratic culture" is avoided. The significant thing is that in the third quarter of the century even the elaborate sermon becomes plain, and it becomes plain very consciously; for the number of works that recommend plain preaching in Anglican pulpits is quite remarkable. An early plea is found in John Wilkins' *Ecclesiastes* of 1646, but most of them appear in the 1660's and 1670's: a sermon of South's preached at Christ Church on April 30, 1668; John Eachard's witty *The Grounds and Occasions of the Contempt of the Clergy and Religion Enquired into* (1670); James Arderne's *Directions concerning the Matter and Style of Sermons* (1671); Herbert Croft's *The Naked Truth* (1675); Joseph Glanvill in more than one work but especially in his *Essay concerning Preaching* (1678); and many another. Some of these men, but not all, were fellows of the Royal Society or had ties with it. Two I will mention, both indifferent or even hostile to the society, Robert South and Herbert Croft, Bishop of Hereford.

South is one of the most vigorous of the Restoration preachers. I said in my first lecture that by the end of the century heresy was no longer hidden and solitary, and heretics were among the objects of his wrath as well as nonconformists and republicans. His armory included scorn, humor, ridicule, the confidence that comes to a man with opinions clearly and firmly held, the advantage of a trenchant style. His sermon on "Christianity Mysterious and the Wisdom of God in making it so" is an attack upon the Socinians. It begins, after the announcement of his text: "The two great works which God has been pleased to signalize his infinite wisdom and power by, were the creation of the world and the redemption of mankind." No teasing of the text here. He plunges into the matter without delay. The rough vigor of his style is indicated by the position of the preposition "by." Tillotson would have written: "The two great works *by* which . . . ," not "The two great works which God has been pleased to signalize his infinite wisdom and power by. . . ." It has been said that Dryden was led by the example of Tillotson to correct his style and in particular to change any sentences that ended with a preposition, in some ways a foolish and unnecessary procedure.

In 1668, a year after Taylor's death, South preached a sermon on plainness of style. The apostles, he said, used a plain, easy, obvious, and familiar style,

> no affected Scheme, or airy Fancies, above the Reach or Relish of an ordinary Apprehension; no, nothing of all this; but their grand Subject was Truth, and consequently above all these petty Arts, and poor Additions; as not being capable of any greater Lustre or Advantage, than to appear just as it is. For there is a certain Majesty in Plainness; as the Proclamation of a Prince never frisks it in Tropes, or fine Conceits, in numerous and well-turned Periods, but *Commands* in sober, natural Expressions.

In St. Paul's manner of preaching he says scornfully—and the reference to Taylor is clear—"Nothing here of the *fringes of the North Star; . . .* nothing of the *down of angels' wings,* or *the beautiful locks of cherubims:* no starched similitudes, introduced with a *Thus have I seen a cloud rolling in its airy mansion,* and the like. No, these were sublimities above the rise of the apostolic spirit." I

suppose we may call this plain as we may call Richard
Sibbes plain, but it is plainness with a difference. Put beside
Taylor it is certainly plain. South is to Taylor as twopence
plain is to penny colored.

The other attack on elaborate preaching I will mention
is Croft's pamphlet *The Naked Truth,* published anonymously. His main argument is that Protestants differ about
nothing essential in religion, and the appearance of such
an argument at such a time was, says Anthony Wood, "like
a comet." It called forth rejoinders and surrejoinders. (Marvell's *Dr. Smirke: or the Divine in Mode* was a surrejoinder.)
There is a section on preaching, attacking those who preach
not in demonstration of the spirit but in demonstration of
their learning, preachers who take a sentence of Scripture,
divide it and subdivide it into generals and particulars,

> the *quid,* the *quale,* the *quantum,* and such like quak-
> salving forms; then they study how to hook in this or
> that quaint sentence of Philosopher or Father, this or
> that nice speculation, endeavouring to couch all this
> in most elegant language; . . . I know full well this
> unapostolick way of Preaching was used by some of
> the Ancient Fathers, especially the *Greeks,* always
> fond of nicities and curiosities, and being now become
> Christians . . . transplanted their beloved Rhetorical
> flowers of humane Learning into Christian gardens.

In this most provocative pamphlet Croft infuriated some
vested interests by maintaining that much of university
learning was useless to a spiritual pastor, that many Masters
of Arts were but schoolboys in true divinity, and that thou-
sands of men in every county of England were as ignorant

as heathens and could understand no more of most sermons
than if they were in Greek.

But let us look for a moment not at attacks on sermons
but at a sermon, and one by the Dr. John North whose life
by his brother Roger I have spoken of. He preached a sermon before Charles II on October 8, 1671, at Newmarket.
It is clear, plain, and short, as Charles II liked his sermons.
I will not say that North never "mentions hell to ears polite,"
but certainly a dissolute or profane person—and the sermon
is about dissolute and profane persons—could listen to such
a preacher without feeling a conviction of sin or even a
passing twinge. It was not so when Latimer or Andrewes
or Donne preached at court. In a turn of speech appropriate
to his audience and to Newmarket the preacher argues that
even if we grant to the profane odds of ten, nay a hundred,
to one on their side against religion, yet the chances of lying
under an eternal torture are so hideous no prudent man
would run the hazard.

The prudential North was not an eminent preacher. The
eminent preachers of his time were South, Barrow, and
Tillotson. It is not surprising that Johnson thought highly
of South. He was a man of robust common sense, of un-
common vigor of mind, of most masculine fancy, fertile in
pithy, homely imagery, a man who might have become a
considerable satirist if he had turned his talents that way.
It would do South no harm in Johnson's opinion that he was
a royalist, a high Anglican, and a Tory. Isaac Barrow, who
before his death at the early age of forty-seven made himself
eminent as mathematician, classical scholar, and divine,
seems to have preached little, yet he wrote many sermons,

some of which he revised four or five times over. He is a considerable writer rather than a considerable preacher; with him as never with Andrewes and Donne, we feel remote from the spoken word. Charles II was of the opinion, and Tillotson agreed, that Barrow was an unfair preacher, because he exhausted every topic, and left no room for anything new to be said by anyone who came after him.

Tillotson, so much admired in his day and for long after his day, is now I suppose unread. He has every virtue and but one vice, the vice of being dull. All the negative praise that Burnet gives Tillotson in his funeral sermon we can agree with: no pomp of words, no superfluities and needless enlargements, no long and affected periods, no affectations of learning, no squeezing of texts, no superficial strains, no false thoughts, no bold flights. But then Burnet proceeds to say that Tillotson was lively. Grant him propriety, clarity, concinnity, solidity, but not liveliness. By his day the pulpit had been purged of much gross pedantry and windy rhetoric, but it had also been purged of eloquence. The splendor departs as well as the pedantry. What remains is plain, clear, direct, rational, and something hardly distinguishable from the moral essay. The great days of pulpit oratory are over.

Notes

PAGES 1–2 Among the books to which I am indebted in this opening lecture, and especially in the opening paragraph, are: Douglas Bush, *English Literature in the Earlier Seventeenth Century, 1600–1660* (Oxford, 1945); P. Hazard, *La Crise de la conscience européene (1680–1715)* (3 vols.; Paris, 1935; English trans., 1953); and Carl Becker, *The Heavenly City of the Eighteenth-Century Philosophers* (3d ed.; New Haven, 1935).

PAGE 3 J. B. Bury, *The Idea of Progress* (London, 1920); R. F. Jones, *Ancients and Moderns* (St. Louis, 1936), chap. ii.

PAGE 3 Raleigh, *History of the World* (1614), I.1.6.9.

PAGE 4 *the advancement of learning in the sixteenth century.* See, for example, F. R. Johnson, *Astronomical Thought in Renaissance England* (Baltimore, 1937). In Louis Le Roy's *De la Vicissitude* (1575), a passage from which in Robert Ashley's translation of 1594 is cited at page 298, there is the same optimism as in Bacon, the same insistence on experiment and observation in testing all knowledge, the same doctrine that the modern age was not surpassed by the greatest ages of antiquity and perhaps surpassed them, and the same belief that man was on the threshold of a new world the key to which was in his hands and the entrance into which would confer untold benefits upon mankind. Here in Ashley's translation (sig. Z1ᵛ) is the title of the great work which Bacon was to publish nine years later: "There was neuer age more happie for the aduancement of learning, then this present. . . . All the mysteries of God and secrets of nature, are not discouered at one time. The greatest things are difficult, and long in comming. How many are there, not as yet reduced into art? How many haue bin first knowen and found out in this age? I say, new lands, new seas, new formes of men, maners, lawes, and customes; new diseases, and new remedies; new waies of the Heauen, and of the Ocean, neuer before found out; and new starres seen? yea, and how many remaine to be knowen by our posteritie? That which is now hidden, with time will come to light; and our successours will wonder that wee were ignorant of them.

PAGE 4   Glanvill, *Scepsis Scientifica* (1665), sig. c1ᵛ.

PAGE 5   *progress or "proficience."* The *Oxford English Dictionary's* earliest example of "progress" in the sense of continuous improvement is dated 1603.

PAGE 5   The quotation is from *The Advancement of Learning* (1605), p. 44ᵛ, in J. M. Robertson, ed., *The Philosophical Works of Francis Bacon* (London, 1905), p. 74.

PAGE 6   On Margaret Blagge (Mrs. Godolphin), see W. G. Hiscock, *John Evelyn and Mrs. Godolphin* (London, 1951), p. 113.

PAGE 7   The letter of 1665 (Oct. 19) is from D. De Repas to Sir Robert Harley, Historical Manuscripts Commission, *Portland Manuscripts*, III (1894), 293.

PAGE 7   *Johnson could say.* See *Journal of a Tour to the Hebrides* (1785), pp. 55–56.

PAGE 8   For Dryden on the English court see W. P. Ker,
ed., *Essays of John Dryden* (2 vols.; Oxford, 1900), I, 176,
and on his own conversation and humor, see *ibid.*, I, 116.
For Sprat's views see his *History of the Royal Society*
(1667), pp. 40–41.

PAGE 8   *raillery.* The word was borrowed from the French
in the early 1650's: see the *Oxford English Dictionary*
under "raillery" and "rallery." In his character "Of Raillery" in *Enigmatical Characters* (1658), no. 15, Flecknoe
—the victim of Dryden's bludgeon if not of his rapier—
draws an elaborate distinction between raillery and satire,
between which there is the same difference "as betwixt
gallantry and clownishness . . . 'tis a plant grows more
naturally in your *Southern* Regions, and seldom farther
North than *Paris* yet: . . . the common People . . . understanding *railing* far better than *Raillery.*" Dryden's
classic passage on "fine raillery" is in the "Discourse of
Satire" prefixed to his translation of Juvenal (1693), but
near the opening of the *Essay of Dramatic Poesy* (1668)
he attacks a poet (Robert Wild?) for his "clenches upon
words, and a certain clownish kind of raillery."

PAGE 9   *Rabelais.* The English translation, *Pantagruel's
Prognostication,* was reprinted by the Luttrell Society in
1947. The quotation is from pages 3–4.

PAGE 10   *The society recommended.* Sprat, *op. cit.*, p. 113.

PAGE 10   *Coleridge.* T. M. Raysor, ed., *Coleridge's Shake-
spearean Criticism* (Cambridge, 1930), I, 149.

PAGE 11   A. B. Walkley, *Dramatic Criticism* (London,
1903), p. 54.

PAGE 12   *I have argued elsewhere.* See my *Elizabethan and
Jacobean* (Oxford, 1945).

PAGE 13   *The paradox.* The quotations are from "The

Mountebank's Masque" in which Paradox appears as a character (A. H. Bullen, ed., *The Works of John Marston* [London, 1887], III, 427); and P. Holland's "explanation of certain obscure words" at the end of his translation of Plutarch's *Moralia* (1603), sig. 5Z5^v. The passage from Hobbes is cited in the *Oxford English Dictionary*.

PAGE 13 For the vogue of the character in the seventeenth century see Gwendolen Murphy, *A Bibliography of Character-Books, 1608–1700* (Oxford, 1925), and C. N. Greenough, *A Bibliography of the Theophrastan Character in English* (Cambridge, 1947).

PAGE 13 Flecknoe, *A Collection of the choicest Epigrams and Characters* (1673).

PAGE 13 Ralph Johnson, *The Scholar's Guide from the Accidence to the University* (1665), p. 15.

PAGE 16 *a branch of lexicography.* In *The Library* (June, 1945), I gave a list of twenty-one collections of proverbs printed between 1640 and 1670, that is, between the collection of 1640 known as George Herbert's and John Ray's of 1670. Some of these were reprinted more than once during the period. To this list should be added: (1) J. Gough, *Academy of Compliments* (1650), pp. 259–264; (2) the 235 numbered Italian proverbs with their English equivalents printed in an appendix to G. Torriano's *Vocabolario Italiano & Inglese, A Dictionary Italian & English* (1659), a revision and enlargement of Florio's *Dictionary*.

PAGE 17 *a step or two nearer to Jonathan Swift.* So we are, too, with the prose of Andrew Marvell, a writer who eschewed the railing of his arrogant adversaries and reduced them and their doctrines to the proper size by the brilliant use of colloquialisms and homely similes. But the style is not well sustained, and not many today will subscribe to Swift's opinion ("Apology" before *A Tale of a Tub*) that "we still read Marvell's Answer to Parker with pleasure, though the book it answers be sunk long ago." Yet the humanity of many of the serious passages is beyond praise, none more so than his courageous defense of Milton (*The Rehearsal Transposed,* Part II [1673], pp. 377–380) against the "scaramuccios" of Parker.

PAGE 19   E. Sackville-West, *Inclinations* (London, 1949), pp. 10–12.

PAGE 19   For advertisements of Deloney's *Gentle Craft* and *Thomas of Reading* in the early eighteenth century, see L. B. Wright, *Midde-Class Culture in Elizabethan England* (Chapel Hill, 1935), pp. 88–89. Greene's *Dorastus and Fawnia* (i.e., *Pandosto*) survived as a chapbook. It was read by the cookmaid in *Clarissa* (1751 ed., IV, 166, letter xxvi).

PAGE 20   *Lamb.* Letter to Wordsworth, Aug. 9, 1815.

PAGE 20   *A father complained.* See Stephen Penton's *The Guardian's Instruction* (1688), 1697 ed., p. 63; reprinted in L. M. Quiller-Couch, ed., *Reminiscences of Oxford, by Oxford Men* (Oxford, 1892), p. 49.

PAGE 21   *Dorothy Osborne.* G. C. Moore Smith, ed., *The Letters of Dorothy Osborne to William Temple* (Oxford, 1928), p. 143.

PAGE 21   *Johnson.* See his *Dictionary* (1755); for Chesterfield's remark see his *Letters* (London, 1774), I, 130.

PAGE 23   On the distinction between Defoe's novels and picaresque fiction see Ernest Bernbaum, *The Mary Carleton Narratives, 1663–1673* (Cambridge, 1914).

PAGE 23 *Queen Victoria.* See her *Diary,* Dec. 23, 1838.

PAGE 24 *"The knowledge of things, not words."* See Daniel Defoe, *The Compleat English Gentleman,* ed. K. D. Bülbring (London, 1890), pp. 209, 212. Other examples of the doctrine are given by A. C. Howell, *"Res et Verba:* Words and Things," *ELH,* XIII (June, 1946), 131–142.

PAGE 24 George Eliot, *Middlemarch,* chap. xv.

PAGE 24 Fielding's letter to Richardson was printed by E. L. McAdam, Jr., in *Yale Review,* XXXVIII (Dec., 1948), 300–310.

PAGE 26 *The Advancement of Learning* (1605), sig. 2X4, in Robertson, *op. cit.,* p. 144.

PAGES 27–28 *Roger North's mother.* See *Life of Sir Dudley North and Dr. John North* (1744), p. 281.

PAGE 31 For Democritus at the haven of Abdera see the *Anatomy* (1638), p. 2. The anecdote about the Thames bargemen first appears in White Kennett's *Register and Chronicle* (1728), p. 320. It continues: "Yet in his College and Chamber so mute and mopish that he was suspected to be *Felo de se,"* a statement at odds with Anthony Wood's well-known and more authoritative one (*Athenae Oxonienses,* ed. Bliss, II, 653): "As he was by many accounted a severe student, a devourer of authors, a melancholy and humorous person; so by others, who knew him well, a person of great honesty, plain dealing and charity. I have heard some of the antients of Christ Church often say that his company was very merry, facete and juvenile, and no man in his time did surpass him for his ready and dextrous interlarding his common discourses among them with verses from the poets or sentences from classical authors. Which being then all the fashion in the university, made his company more acceptable."

PAGE 33   The couplet is John Speed's; verses prefixed to
E. Gayton's *Pleasant Notes upon Don Quixote* (1654),
sig. **I^v.

PAGES 33–34   C. H. Firth, ed., *The History of England, by
Lord Macaulay* (6 vols.; London, 1914), IV, 1724. Perhaps
Macaulay would not have been so severe if Dodwell had
not been a nonjuror.

PAGE 34   The quotation in reduced type is from the edition
of 1638 (2.2.4, p. 266), the last to appear in Burton's lifetime.

PAGE 34   *perhaps by way of an Elizabethan intermediary.*
Not intending an edition of Burton I have not examined
all the Elizabethan books on fishing. The passage is in
William Gryndall's *Hawking, Hunting, Fowling, and Fishing* (1596), sig. I4^v, but Burton is in places nearer to the
text of 1496.

PAGE 45   The Osler quotation is from Oxford Bibliographical Society, *Proceedings* (1926), Vol. I, Part III, p. 184.

PAGE 48   *"lean-to."* The word is found in R. Harris' *Samuel's
Funeral, or a sermon preached at the funeral of Sir Anthony Cope* (*Works*, 1634–35), and is cited by William
Haller, *The Rise of Puritanism* (New York, 1938), pp. 101,
385. Haller gives valuable bibliographical notes on this
kind of literature.

PAGE 48   *"accepted with the Saints."* Clarke's *Lives of Sun-
dry Eminent Persons in this Later Age* (1683), Preface.

PAGE 51   Sisson, *The Judicious Marriage of Mr Hooker*
(Cambridge, Eng., 1940).

PAGE 54   John Butt, "Izaak Walton's Collections for Ful-
man's Life of John Hales," *Modern Language Review*,
XXIX (1934), 267–273. Also of importance is his essay
on Walton's methods in biography, *Essays and Studies of*

the English Association, XIX (1934), 67–84. David Novarr's full and valuable study, *The Making of Walton's "Lives"* (Ithaca, 1958), has appeared since my lecture was prepared. The Walton who emerges "is neither so peaceable nor so honest nor so simple as has been frequently thought, but he is one who gains in stature as we see his concern for craftsmanship and his involvement in the prime issues of his time" (p. x).

PAGE 55   Milton, *The History of Britain, That part especially now call'd England* (1670), p. 66. But the doctrine had been expressed in English almost a century earlier. See T. Blundeville, *The true order and method of writing and reading Histories* (1574), edited by Hugh G. Dick in *Huntington Library Quarterly,* III (Jan., 1940), 164: "the hystoriographers ought not to fayne anye Orations nor any other thing, but truely to reporte euery such speach, and deede, euen as it was spoken, or done." Blundeville is following the Italian historiographer Francesco Patrizi, whose *Della Historia Diece Dialoghi* was published at Venice in 1560.

PAGE 56   *the table talk of eminent men.* I repeat a few phrases from my article on "Table Talk," *Huntington Library Quarterly,* IV (Oct., 1940), 27–46.

PAGE 57   *of him it has been said.* David Masson, *Life of Milton,* I (1881), 525.

PAGE 57   *Plutarch.* It is significant that Dryden's praise of biography comes in his life of Plutarch, a writer who held that sometimes a word or a jest is more revealing than a battle or the sack of a city. See *Plutarch's Lives Translated . . . by Several Hands,* I (1683), 93–94. Dryden observes that, unlike annals and history, biography admits "a descent into minute circumstances, and trivial passages of life": "There you are conducted only into the rooms of state; here you are led into the private Lodgings of the Heroe: you see him in his undress, and are made Familiar with his most private actions and conversations. You may behold a *Scipio* and a *Lelius* gathering Cockle-shells on the shore, *Augustus* playing at bounding stones with Boyes; and *Agesilaus* riding on a Hobby-horse among his Children. The Pageantry of Life is taken away; you see the poor reasonable Animal, as naked as ever nature made him; are made acquainted with his passions and his follies, and find the *Demy-God* a *Man*."

PAGE 59   The quotation in reduced type is from *Wiltshire. The Topographical Collections of John Aubrey, F.R.S.,* ed. J. E. Jackson (1862), p. 17.

PAGE 62   *what an enemy said about it.* See *An Appendix to the Life of Seth Lord Bishop of Salisbury . . . in a Letter to the Author* (1697), pp. 3–5, 34. Published anonymously, it is by Thomas Wood, Anthony Wood's nephew.

PAGES 65–66   The quotations in reduced type are from Roger North's *Life of Francis North Baron of Guilford* (1742), p. 77, from his *Life of Sir Dudley North and Dr. John North* (1744), p. 239, and from Jonathan Richardson's *Explanatory Notes and Remarks on Milton's Paradise Lost* (1734), prefatory note.

PAGE 66   *he lay with his Tutor:* a practice long since abandoned in the two ancient universities of England.

PAGE 68   Emerson, *English Traits,* chap. xiv, "Literature."

PAGE 69   *"sense of musical delight."* See *Biographia Literaria,* chap. xv.

PAGE 71   *Harington.* See the notes at the end of his translation of *Orlando Furioso,* book xxxiv.

PAGE 72   The quotation in reduced type is from *Medicus Medicatus,* p. 35.

PAGE 74   For the quotation in reduced type, see G. L.

Keynes, ed., *The Works of Sir Thomas Browne* (6 vols.; London, 1928–1931), I, 43.

PAGE 75   Bacon, *The Advancement of Learning* (1605), sig. 212^v, in Robertson, *op. cit.*, p. 100.

PAGE 76   The quotations are from *King John*, V.vii.21; *Hamlet*, IV.v.143; and *The Phoenix and Turtle*.

PAGE 78   The quotation in reduced type is from Ross's *Arcana Microcosmi* (1651), p. 292. Ross died in 1654. The year before, he attacked Hobbes in *Leviathan drawn out with a hook*. Hobbes had his revenge in his *Of Liberty and Necessity* (1654), sig. A8, where he says that Ross had so much learning that he was "perpetually barking at the works of the most learned." There is more to be said for Ross's guide to Greek and Roman mythology, *Mystagogus Poeticus, or the Muses' Interpreter*, published in 1647 and often reprinted, which at Harvard College was thought more convenient than Natalis Comes, though not so large. Cf. S. E. Morison, *The Founding of Harvard College* (Cambridge, 1935), p. 68.

PAGE 79   *"twilight of the medieval gods."* W. P. Dunn, *Sir Thomas Browne* (Minneapolis, 1950), p. 6.

PAGE 81   *"unicorn's horn."* For this and other early experiments see T. Birch, *History of the Royal Society* (1756), I, 41, 66, and C. R. Weld, *History of the Royal Society* (1848), I, 110–113. On the circle of pure unicorn's horn charming what is within it, see John Webster's *The White Devil*, II.i.268.

PAGE 82   John Evelyn, *Diary,* ed. E. S. de Beer (Oxford, 1955), III, 592–594.

PAGE 82   John Ray, *A Collection of English Words* (1674), Preface. The catalogue of English birds is on pages 81–96.

PAGE 82   *Lord Keeper Guilford.* See Roger North's *Life* (1742), p. 285.

PAGES 83–84   For the quotations from Browne's letters see
Keynes, *op. cit.*, VI, 48, 333, 237, 28.

PAGE 84   *Huntley.* See *Studies in Philology*, LIII (1956),
204–219.

PAGE 84   Ross, *Medicus Medicatus*, p. 79: ". . . 'tis not out
of a humour of contradiction or vainglory, nor of any
intention I have to bring you or your Booke into obloquie,
that I have marked out its obliquities."

PAGE 88   For Manningham see his *Diary*, ed. J. Bruce
(1868), pp. 75, 84–85, 104–105, 132.

PAGE 89   On Rainolds' memory and reading see Joseph
Hall, *Epistles* (1608), Decade 1, Epistle 7, p. 72.

PAGES 90–91   Evidence of the length of sermons is given
by W. Matthews in *The Library*, XV (1934–35), 496–497.
On Barrow see W. Pope, *Life of Seth Ward* (1697), pp.
146–148. The anecdote about Chaderton is told in Dr. Dil-
lingham's life of him, translated in 1884 by E. S. Shuck-
burgh, page 13. For Meriton see his *Sermon of Nobility*
(1607), sig. A4, and for George Montaigne see N. E. Mc-
Clure, ed., *The Letters of John Chamberlain* (Philadelphia, 1939), II, 470. The passage from Fleming's *Lamb*
is on sig. D4^v. George Herbert held that "the Parson ex-
ceeds not an hour in preaching, because all ages have
thought that a competency, and he that profits not in that
time, will less afterwards" (F. E. Hutchinson, ed., *The
Works of George Herbert* [Oxford, 1941], p. 235). See
also the next note.

PAGE 91   *Paul's Cross.* Millar MacLure's excellent study,
The Paul's Cross Sermons, 1534–1642 (Toronto, 1958),
was published after the delivery of this lecture. He gives
a good bibliography. A letter sent by the Bishop of London
to a clergyman (unknown) instructing him to preach at
the Cross survives in Rawl. MS D. 399, fol. 115: "Salutem

in Christo. You shall understand that you are appointed
to preach at St Paul's Crosse on Sunday the 29 of Nouem-
ber next ensuinge, by discreet performance whereof you
shall doe good seruice to God, the King's Ma:^{tie}, and the
Church. These are therefore to require and charge you
not to faile of your day appointed, and to send your
answer of acceptance hereof in writing to my Chaplaine
Dr Wykes at London House, and to bring a Coppie of your
Sermon wth you, and not to exceed an hour and an halfe
in both Sermon and Praier. As also to Certifie y[our]
presence sometime on the Thursday before your day appointed to John Flemming Draper in Watlingstreet, at
whose House your entertainment is prouided. And hereof
faile not as you will answe[r] the Contrarie at your perill.
Your louinge Freind Guil. London." The signature is William Juxon's, not William Laud's as the printed catalogue
of the Rawlinson Manuscripts says. Juxon succeeded Laud
as Bishop of London in 1633. November 29 fell on a Sunday in 1635 and 1640. As Thomas Wykes did not proceed
D.D. till 1639 (Wood, *Fasti*, ed. Bliss, I, 510), the year of
the letter appears to be 1640.

PAGES 91–92   For a subject analysis of books printed before 1641 see E. L. Klotz in the *Huntington Library Quarterly*, I (1937–38), 417–419; and for a bibliography of
Elizabethan sermons see A. F. Kerr, *The Elizabethan
Sermon, a Survey and a Bibliography* (Philadelphia,
1940).

PAGE 92   For the quotation in reduced type see the Preface,
1638 edition, p. 15.

PAGE 93   *"a distinct judgement . . ."* Joseph Hall, *op. cit.*,
p. 72.

PAGE 94   *a preacher at Paul's Cross.* T. W. (Thomas

White?), A *Sermon . . . in time of the Plague* (1578), p. 46.

PAGE 94   A. B. Grosart, ed., *The Complete Works in Verse and Prose of Andrew Marvell* (4 vols.; London, 1872–1875), III, 192.

PAGE 96   For South see the sermon referred to in the note to page 107; for Pococke see W. F. Mitchell, *English Pulpit Oratory from Andrewes to Tillotson* (London, 1932), p. 106; and for Aylmer see Strype's life of him (1701), p. 30.

PAGE 98   The quotation in reduced type is from Donne's *LXXX Sermons* (1640), Sermon II, p. 13.

PAGE 101   *Felton.* Fuller, *Worthies* (1662), *s.v.* London, p. 206.

PAGE 103   On the simile of the silkworm in Elizabeth Grymeston and Taylor see G. Bone in *The Library*, 4th series, XV (1935), 247–248. For Saint Teresa's elaborate comparison of the spiritual life with the natural life of the silkworm, see E. A. Peers, trans. and ed., *The Complete Works of Saint Teresa of Jesus* (London, 1946), II, 253–254.

PAGE 103   *jeremitaylorically.* The adverb is Peacock's: *Nightmare Abbey*, chap. viii.

PAGE 103   Henry Crosse, *Virtue's Commonwealth* (1603), sig. O2ᵛ.

PAGE 106   On the changes in pulpit style see the valuable studies by R. F. Jones, *The Seventeenth Century* (Stanford, 1951), pp. 111–142, and G. Williamson, *The Senecan Amble* (Chicago, 1951), chap. 8.

PAGE 107   South's sermon may be found in *Twelve Sermons and Discourses* (6th ed.; 1727), V. See pp. 434–436.

Index of Names